Parables & the Enneagram

Parables
and the
Enneagram

By
Clarence Thomson

Metamorphous Press
Portland, OR

Metamorphous Press
P.O. Box 10616
Portland, OR 97296-0616
503-228-4972

Scripture quotations are from the Revised Standard Version

Printed in the United States

Library of Congress Cataloing-in Publication Data

Thomson, Clarence, 1935 -
      Parables and the enneagram / Clarence Thomson
        p. cm.
      ISBN 1-55552-106-7
      1. Jesus Christ---Parables. 2. Enneagram. I. Title
BT375.2.T53   1996
226.8.'06'-19----dc20   96-10517
                            CIP

$\int$

To my wife Patricia,

for gracefully yielding garden time
so I could do this,

& my sisters,
Sheila and Becky,

whose encouragement was
as irresistible as Spring

Acknowledgments

My first debt is to Tom Condon, whose writings have graced my Enneagram Educator newsletter since I attended my first Enneagram workshop with him in Oregon several years ago. My debt is general—he has deepened and clarified my understanding of the Enneagram in myriad ways. The debt is also specific: In a fine throwaway line, he once characterized the secondary gain of addiction as a "booby prize." This understanding shows up in my distinction between what each type wants and what he or she will settle for. Each type settles for a "booby prize," instead of getting what she or he really wants. Condon also originated the idea that each type has a specific set of actions—a strategy—that generates the Enneagram style, moment by moment.

I owe Megan McKenna a debt of thanks for letting me use several of her stories. Traces of some of her audiocassette versions also show up in my retellings of the parables of the breaking of the bread and the wicked king who gives talents and demands interest on them.

I'm grateful to John Pilch for keeping me abreast of some of the latest developments in Scripture scholarship. I learned about the Roman law that I mention in the chapter on Eights from him in his Credence Cassette series, Stories Your Pastor Never Told You.

And thanks to Mike Leach, my publisher, whose idea this was in the first place. Sometimes one doesn't dance until asked.

Contents

Foreword

Recently on the television news there was a report about a conflict between the mascots of two sports teams. One mascot was a man in a bear costume while the other was dressed as a tree. During a game an altercation began when the bear insulted the tree's team. The tree grew angry and threw a punch.

In response, the bear shoved the tree and soon the two were on the ground trading blows. The police arrested both the bear and the tree and booked them into jail. The straightfaced reporter went on to say that charges were dropped after the tree agreed to make a public apology to the bear.

This incident underscores something the Enneagram illustrates in its comprehensive, penetrating way: that our reactions to events are often metaphorical. We live out of scripts and stories but forget the fact, often confusing our outer costumes for our inner selves.

As Clarence Thomson says in this artful, fascinating book, the scripts we live are necessary. They help us maintain our daily world and selectively filter reality even as they induce in us a kind of open-eyed hypnotic trance. Within the trance of our Enneagram story we see ourselves and reality in one basic way, which is correct as far as it goes. But we are also closed to other realms, especially numinous, transcendent ones.

Therapeutic metaphor is a well-studied communication technique. Priests, psychotherapists, and teachers all tell stories to help people expand the limits of their personal scripts. In this book, Thomson persuasively argues that the parables of Jesus are more than metaphors; they are trance-breaking interventions designed to minister to core dilemmas, especially the kind described by the Enneagram.

Parables and the Enneagram does a great service by unraveling the teachings of Jesus in ways that will appeal to Christians and non-Christians alike. It also broadens the Enneagram by deftly and intelligently applying the system. Thomson presents the parable not only for its spiritual power but as a literary and therapeutic form. For this and many other reasons, *Parables* will find a wide audience in seekers and clinicians of all kinds.

—Thomas Condon

Introduction

BREAKING THE TRANCE

Once upon a time, a long time ago, there was a king in Ireland. Ireland had lots of small kingdoms in those days, and this king's kingdom was one among many. Both king and kingdom were quite ordinary and nobody paid much attention to either of them.

But one day, the king received a huge beautiful diamond from a relative who had died. It was the largest diamond anyone had ever seen. It dazzled everyone. The other kings began to pay attention to him for if he had a diamond like this he must be special. The people, too, came from far and wide to see the diamond. The king had it on constant display in a glass box so that all who wished could come to see and admire it. Of course, armed guards kept a constant vigil. Both king and kingdom prospered, and the king attributed all his good fortune to the diamond.

One day a nervous guard asked to see him. The guard was visibly shaken. He told the king terrible news: the diamond had developed a flaw! A crack right down the middle! The king was horrified and ran to the glass box to see for himself. It was true. The diamond was now flawed terribly.

He called all the jewelers in the land to ask their advice. They gave him only bad news. The flaw was so deep, they said, that if they were to try to sand it down, they would grind it to practically nothing, and if they tried to split it into two still substantial stones, it easily might shatter into a million fragments.

As the king was pondering these terrible options, an old jeweler who had arrived late came to him and said, "If you will give me a week with that stone, I think I can fix it." The king didn't believe him at first because the other jewelers were so sure it couldn't be fixed, but the old man was insistent. Finally the king relented, but said he couldn't let the diamond out of his castle. The old man said that would be all right: He could work there and the guards could stand outside the room where he was working.

The king, having no better solution, agreed to let the old man work. For a week he and the guards hovered about, hearing scratching and gentle pounding and grinding. They wondered what he was doing and what would happen if the old man were tricking them.

Finally, the week was up and the old man came out of the room. King and guards rushed in to see the man's work, and the king burst into tears of joy. It *was* better! The old man had carved a perfect rose on the top of the diamond, and the crack that ran down inside now was the stem of the rose.

When the Irish tell this story, they say that this is the way God heals us. He takes our deepest flaw and turns it—and us—into something beautiful.

The Enneagram is about our flaws. Each of us has one serious flaw that shapes our personality. This flaw is called our Enneagram style, or type, in most Enneagram literature, and I would add that this flaw is also our Enneagram strategy.

Our flaw is, first of all, a distorted vision of the world—and a correspondingly skewed view of God, for these wrong viewpoints or attitudes are usually the same. Thus our flaw is a strategy for dealing with God and this world that we see through a murky and distorted lens.

Our flaw is our Enneagram type. It has strengths and weaknesses, but the strengths are really by-products of the weaknesses, like the powerful muscles a person in a wheel chair sometimes develops: powerful, but compensatory rather than integral.

If we do any one thing too much, we tend to become unbalanced, but even in our imbalance, we develop certain skills, aptitudes, and strategies. A criminal may know more law than many lawyers. It is usually a distortion, but it is also a talent. Someone addicted to comic books as a child may make a fortune trading them later in life because she knows the field intimately. This is how the Enneagram energy works. When someone has a passion for anything, she learns how to satisfy it.

So our Enneagram style is our flaw, our chief distortion. How shall we carve the rose?

This book is filled with suggestions, but one generalization covers them all and needs some explanation: People of faith believe that reading scripture is good for them. Some believe it more strongly than others, but millions go to church services each week and have the Scriptures read to them. How does that help them?

Underlying this widespread behavior is a usually poorly defined or inarticulate belief that such listening will make them more spiritual. Part of this belief is our naïve notion that the Scriptures are "answers," and if we go to church, such answers will be read to us out of the book. Indeed, Billy Graham has referred to the Bible as "God's answer book."

Some of us don't think that's how it works. And if someone, in innocent eagerness, turns to his or her Enneagram type number looking for the answer to what's wrong with him or her, I can promise a sustained disappointment.

Scriptures mold us subtly, over a period of time, like any other story. We see the mechanism at work by those geniuses of behavior modification, advertisers. When they sell a little kid a T-shirt with Michael Jordan's number on it, they are changing the way that little kid thinks about himself. They are changing his inner world. When the kid walks onto the court to shoot baskets, he unconsciously adopts the values, styles, mannerisms—whatever he can— of his hero. In a certain sense, he becomes the person he admires. The content in this case may be trivial, but the process is not.

The process is shaping through imagination. Imagination is where our power to change—to carve the rose—lies.

Advertisers do not reason with us; they capture our imagination. Many people foolishly argue that "I'm not influenced by television because the ads don't make sense." But there are too many dollars and brains involved for advertisers to bother with rational persuasion. They know better. They appeal to our imagination.

The appeal to the imagination is in direct contrast to two other ways of trying to bring about change. The first is the above-mentioned appeal to reason: "Just stop being bad and start being good. Don't be so compulsive and stop worrying." We've all heard this kind of talk. Therapists, teachers, moms, dietitians—everybody's saying it, and we all know it doesn't work. We see lots of this advice in many Enneagram books. "The Four needs to move to One and get in touch with his objectivity and moral principles." That's certainly true, but I wonder why it so seldom happens? Because you don't quarry stone with a razor blade. Simple rational explanations lack power.

Nor does the appeal to will power work. Tell a phobic person to just grit her teeth and forget her foolish fears. The effort only makes it worse. A certain Catholic tradition called *agere contra* still is taught in some retreat houses and books of piety. It means "to act against" and many of the saints told of just doing what they most wanted not to do. There is a certain context in which that can work, like St. Francis kissing the leper, but as a command or an act of the will, it is bound to fail. Ask anyone who has tried to diet by will power.

Jesus took a different tack. He appealed to the imagination. For example, when he heard that John had been beheaded, he went out into the desert to pray and the people followed him in droves. Here's Mark's account:

> **"Come away by yourselves to a lonely place, and *rest a while*." For many were coming and going, and *they had no leisure* even to eat. And they went away *in the boat* to a lonely place by themselves. Now many saw them going, and knew them, and they ran there on foot from all the towns, and got there ahead of them. As he landed he saw a great throng, and he had compassion on them, because they were like *sheep without a shepherd*;**

and he began to teach them many things. And when it
grew late, his disciples came to him and said, "*This is a
lonely place*, and the hour is now late; send them away
to go into the country and villages round about and buy
themselves something to eat." But he answered them,
"You give them something to eat." And they said to him,
"Shall we go and buy two hundred denarii worth of
bread, and give it to them to eat?" And he said to them,
"How many loaves have you? Go and see." And when
they had found out, they said, "Five and two fish." Then
he commanded them all to sit down by companies *upon
the green grass*. So they sat down in groups, *by hundreds
and by fifties*. And taking the five loaves and the two fish
he looked up to heaven, and blessed, and broke the
loaves, and gave them to the disciples to set before the
people; and he divided the two fish among them all.
And they all ate and were satisfied. And they took up
twelve baskets full of broken pieces and of the fish. And
those who ate the loaves were five thousand men.

—Mark 6:31–44

When Mark tells this story to people who know their
Hebrew Scriptures, they recognize that Jesus is acting out Psalm
23. Perhaps the best known of all the Psalms, it begins:

**The Lord is my Shepherd, I shall not want; he makes me
lie down in green pastures.**

—Psalm 23:1

Go back and read the story and notice the words in italics. They
would have been as significant to the people of that day as to
imply, in our own time, that a gathering is political by saying
that everyone wore red, white, and blue.

Mark looks to the previous scriptures for his interpretation. The commands of Jesus to sit down in groups of fifty and
one hundred probably look at the contemporary church which
met in numbers about that size. He looks backward and forward; so should we. We dress our imaginative world with the

images of Scripture and then we live out of that imagination. We often talk about interpreting Scripture; it is even more accurate to say that the stories, images, and sayings of Jesus interpret our lives. Those images answer the question we ask ourselves—and if our behavior is too outrageous, others ask us, "What do you think you're doing?" When Mark wanted to explain to his people what Jesus thought he was doing, he selected well-known scriptural images. That's what I am suggesting: how to use Scripture. The metaphors, parables, and images engage our imagination on a deeper level, where real change happens and the multiplicity and diversity of the images prevent fanaticism and rigidity. If someone lives out of only a few phrases or images, fundamentalism occurs.

The answer to that question, "What do you think you are doing?" is really: "I'm acting out my imagination. I'm acting out who I think I am, who I think God is, and what I think the world is like. The reason my behavior may seem bizarre to you is that you don't know my inner images, the furniture of my mind." The contribution of the Enneagram is to describe the inner geography of each other's minds. The contribution of the Scripture is to offer alternatives to that geography.

TWO VISIONS OF THE WORLD

Our Enneagram vision of the world, regardless of which of the nine it is, is in direct conflict with the vision of Jesus. Jesus puts it this way:

> **No man can serve two masters; for either he will hate the one and love the other, or he will be devoted to the one and despise the other. You cannot serve God and mammon.**
>
> **—Matthew 6:24**

Now Jesus was—as was the prophetical tradition in general—suspicious of the pursuit of wealth. But this is an awfully strong statement. Jesus never made us choose between God and pleasure, or God and power, or God and sex. Just God and money. Why?

I don't know, but I offer this as an educated guess: The first rule of economics is, as any student of Econ 101 should know, "supply and demand." If someone knows only one principle of economics, that's what she knows. And supply and demand, in turn, presupposes a scarcity of goods.

Economics and our Enneagram styles have this in common: They presuppose a world in which there isn't enough of whatever it is that I want. My Enneagram style is a style in which I have to work terribly hard to get what I am utterly devoted to. Sixes try too hard to find security, and Threes will do what it takes to be successful. Each number does something similar.

Against this emotional mind-set—an imaginative construct of scarcity—Jesus opposes his vision of the kingdom of God, where there is plenty: enough of everything to go around. Mark's parable of the breaking of the bread has as its main theological point that in the kingdom there is enough to go around. The lilies of the field, the pearl of great price, many other parables similarly insist that life with God is a life of abundance.

Jesus is not naïve. But he is a mystic. Mystics frequently talk in terms of abundance, of resolution of apparent opposites, of eternal happy endings—regardless of what the present experience is. Jesus sees the world coming from his Father and so whatever comes is just what should be. He teaches us in the Our Father to ask for "daily bread," like the manna that was furnished to the Hebrews in the desert. The tradition is that God will give us what we need: Jesus lives out of that image. Hoarding bread is not only greed; it is lack of faith in the vision of abundance. Where there is abundant love, everything is abundant. The world of money, of economics, is a world of scarcity. You can't operate from a viewpoint of scarcity and one of abundance at the same time. The service of money (which may be radically different than having or not having it) indicates a lack of faith; it is the action that betrays your inner world of scarcity. The reason you can't serve God and money is that worldviews of abundance and scarcity can't coexist.

So the parables of Jesus are confounding because they are descriptions of his inner world flooded with the presence of God—one might say a world without an Enneagram flaw. To the extent our inner world "isn't like that," we will experience the parables as nonsense, just as we might see the behavior of other Enneagram styles as nonsense because we don't share their worldview.

Matthew's Gospel records that when Jesus was preaching the good news, he spoke in parables. As effective as Jesus was in getting everyone's attention and bringing about conversion or hostility, it seems that parables were an especially fine literary form to choose.

Jesus tells us why he spoke in parables:

> **This is why to them I speak in parables, because seeing, they do not see, and hearing, they do not hear, nor do they understand.**
> **—Matthew 13:13**

Jesus speaks in parables because of the inability of his listeners to hear or see. What can he have meant by that? Why talk at all to people who won't hear? Why address people who can't understand?

Because they—and we—are in trances. We are not fully awake, fully present.

Contemporary research reveals more and more about trances, about how we hear and see selectively, hearing only what we want, expect, or need to hear. Several levels of this understanding can be discerned. The first level is common sense. We all know, consciously or unconsciously that most people have "blind spots," about which they get very defensive. There are no people so blind as those who *will* not see. We use phrases like "There's no way he is going to hear that" when we are referring to a person who is decidedly unsympathetic.

Trances are not esoteric, mysterious, or unusual. They are a way of paying attention to a few select things out of all the buzzing multiplicity of life. We all experience trances of one kind or another. I look at things one way at midnight, but in the morning, "Things look different." We say things "look different" because we don't want to admit that we don't see things the way they are. Being very hungry or just having finished a good meal changes one's focus of attention and hierarchy of values dramatically. Samuel Johnson noted that the prospect of being hanged wonderfully focused one's mind! So does almost getting creamed on the freeway.

Few trances equal the hormonally induced focused attention of first love. Fatigue, caffeine, fine wine or cheap bourbon, a company memo that your job might be eliminated, your child calling from the hospital—all these can make parts of your world come into focus and other parts recede instantaneously.

Technically these are trances. They are states of mind in which we focus on one thing—or a few related things—and exclude everything else.

Contemporary therapies, especially the kind using hypnosis developed by Milton Erickson and neuro-linguistic programming, which is loosely associated with it, delve even more deeply into selective hearing and seeing deeper. Erickson used stories, metaphors, and symbolic interventions to change people's lifetime behaviors in a single session. His acknowledged genius for this brought hypnosis into clinical respectability. He made it into a serious tool and thus revealed that we are all hypnotized in some respect but, by changing our hypnotic trance, we can change our lives. Erickson enabled us to comprehend that we can't see really important things if "not seeing" was our way of coping with reality at an earlier age. The word *trance* became a common way of talking about distortions of perception that existed on many levels in many ways. It wasn't some mysterious loss of self or will induced by an outside agent; it was something we did to ourselves so that we didn't have to look at things too frightening or repulsive to handle. Sexual abuse victims report that they can't feel during sexual intercourse. They're in a trance. They feel but don't feel.

But it doesn't take something as extreme as sexual abuse. It can be a cultural habit. Storyteller and scripture scholar Megan McKenna told me this story about herself. She was in Albuquerque, New Mexico, talking with a fellow theologian, who was Native American. They were walking along a busy street, with horns blowing, traffic whizzing, and many people on foot talking, when suddenly her friend remarked, "Listen, hear those crickets?" Megan listened but could not hear. She began to tease her Native friend saying, "I don't hear any crickets! Are you putting me on, saying you can hear what I can't because you are Indian?"

Her friend just grinned and said, "No, follow me." Walking off the sidewalk a few yards, they came to a group of crickets, and once Megan saw them she was able to hear them.

"It's just a matter of what you're listening for," he said. "Watch." Taking a few coins out of his pocket, he threw them on the ground. Everybody within a hundred feet stopped and looked at them.

The people passing were all listening for money. They weren't listening for crickets. Technically, according to hypnotists, they were all in a trance. Likewise, we are all in similar trances, each of our own making and serving our own purposes.

Dr. Stephen Wolinsky, author of the book, *Trances People Live*, is a therapist in the Ericksonian tradition. He argues that not only are we all in trances, cultural and personal, but also that *"trance phenomena are the means by which symptoms are created and maintained."* By this he means that all our neurotic behavior and feelings are rooted in our trances. We don't have neurotic behavior when we see the world the way it really is. If we can find a way to break our trances, we can free ourselves from much painful or destructive behavior and the feelings that lead to this behavior.

To vastly oversimplify his point: As a result of repeated or traumatic events in our past, we stop looking or hearing or feeling. Then we behave in a way appropriate to our truncated and distorted worldview. We keep acting out this earlier state.

A mild cultural example might illustrate this: We've all heard of lottery winners who keep shopping at thrift stores. Why? Because they can't let go of an earlier worldview in which they were poor. When someone is six years old and her father tells her she is stupid, no matter how smart she may become, she may still see herself as stupid. She doesn't see the world as it is; she sees it the way she was told to see it back when she was only six.

Thus healthy, enlightened, and holy people do what works. Unhealthy, neurotic, and sinful people do what used to work.

Notice how dynamic Wolinsky's observation is. We both create and maintain our symptoms through our trances. A trance isn't just a pair of colored glasses through which we see the world; it is a strong suggestion about how to behave in a world like this. As Rollo May dryly observed, "When all you have is a hammer, the whole world looks like a nail." Yes, and if the whole world looks like a nail, why wouldn't you walk through life with a hammer? Unfortunately such thinking is a vicious circle: If we keep hammering on people, they become as hard as nails.

In his advanced workshop on therapy and the Enneagram, Thomas Condon argues that our enneagam type is both a world-view and a strategy. He says our Enneagram strategy is a series of rather rigidly sequenced steps by which we energetically go after what we don't have. The amazing thing is that we go after what we don't have because we gave it away first. For example, a type Six will be driving down the road and a car will pull out in front of him. Six will immediately tell himself that driving is danger-ous and make plans to learn to be a race car driver so as to be safe in this world of crazy traffic. Then, if he does that, *he can have the security that he had before he frightened himself.*

If we are all in some kind of trance and now have the sci-entific tools to examine those trances, then Jesus' decision to talk in parables makes more sense. Parables are a way to talk to peo-ple in trances—a way to talk to people who listen but don't hear, see but don't see, and do not understand.

Parables are a literary form that can bypass our usual defenses and convince us of truths we have been unable to see or hear because of our trances.

Stories can do the same thing, as can a lot of "right-brain" language forms like slogans, proverbs, aphorisms, and metaphors.

Parables are the opposite of stories, however. Parables tell us we are wrong about the way we see the world. They are neg-ative in a logical sense. They tell us that what we always thought was true is not, but they don't tell us what is true. That is an extremely important distinction. Many parables tell us what is not true, but then we have to figure out for ourselves what real-ly is true. In other words, parables tell us that we are wearing distorting lenses, but when we take them off and see things clearly for ourselves, the parable does not then tell us what we are going to see instead.

That's why Jesus used parables: to enable us to see for ourselves. When we can see for ourselves, then we are free. So the relationship between Jesus' coming to set us free and his telling parables is clearer. It is clearer, too, why after telling parables, Jesus promises us to send the Paraclete, the Holy Spirit. The parables teach us to not believe what is false and thus they prepare the way for the Paraclete to teach us what is true.

Parables are profoundly respectful. When Jesus tells us a parable that destroys our entranced view of the world and does not replace it with anything, he clearly has confidence that we can see for ourselves. He doesn't replace the old law with a new one, and he doesn't replace one trance with another. He replaces the trance with reality and tells us to look.

When he does tell us what to think, he speaks to us through stories, not parables. Stories create an inner world for us. All school teachers are required to take courses in the history of a state in which they teach, the sound assumption being that a teacher can communicate better with her students when she knows the geography of their outer world, and can thus approach their inner world more comfortably as well. Stories shape us, tell us what is true, what can be true, and how we act to reflect who we are. But parables have the added power of being able to correct stories that we have misinterpreted.

There's a similar difference between oppressive, cult-like religions—which claim to have all the answers—and what Jesus preached. Cult leaders insist on mind control, but Jesus insists on talking in parables to return the control to us.

A parable says if we could just let go our narrowness, we could see more of the world.

For example, we all know the parable of the Good Shepherd, which has so captured our imagination that parishes, hospitals, convents, and hospices continue to be named after it today:

What do you think? If a man has a hundred sheep, and one of them has gone astray, does he not leave the ninety-nine on the hills and go in search of the one that

went astray? And if he finds it, truly, I say to you, he rejoices over it more than over the ninety-nine that never went astray. So it is not the will of my father who is in heaven that one of these little ones shall perish.

—Matthew 18:12–14

Do not put this man in charge of your day-care center. If you have money, don't let him near your portfolio.

This is *not* good advice on how to be a shepherd. If you left ninety-nine sheep alone, how many would be there when you returned? Of those you found, how many would be alive? If you ran your sophomore religion class and you left the nineteen and went after the one, what would your classroom look like when you returned? And if you were gone twenty minutes, how many would be there?

So what's the point of a parable if it is not good advice?

The point of the parable is that we are wrong about life as we see it. Convincing someone they are fundamentally wrong about life is no small accomplishment. How many people do you know whom you would love to convince that they see things all wrong? How many in public office? If we look within ourselves, we admit that we also have a number of things we "know" are true that really are not. Therapists earn their money if they can convince us to see the world in a different way. And we describe our own growth and conversion process as learning to see what was always there that we simply couldn't see ("I realized for the first time how . . .").

Take the story of the Good Samaritan, which is recounted in Luke 10:25. A lawyer (the man in charge of how things ought to be, the law) asked Jesus what he had to do to be saved. Jesus knew the man already knew the rules, so he asked what was in the law. The lawyer answered correctly, as lawyers are supposed to, and Jesus says, "All right, do that and you will live." But the lawyer—and Luke inserts this telltale phrase—"wishing to justify himself," asks Jesus, "Who is my neighbor?" Jesus is bright; he is not going to get into a discussion of the fine points of the law with a Jewish lawyer. So he tells him the parable of the Good Samaritan.

Why? Why does he tell the parable to the lawyer who already knows how to be saved?

Because he has to break down the lawyer's conceptual world, his trance. We are always self-justifying within the confines of our trance, saying: "If you knew what I knew, you would have done [whatever], . . . too." If Jesus had told the story and made the Jewish priest who also appears in the parable the hero, that would have been taken as good advice by the people: "See? Do as your priest did, and take care of those who need help." The lawyer and the people would have been a lot more likely to follow the example of the priest than that of a Samaritan—a minority despised by Jews in biblical times. But this would have kept them in their trance, which said all Samaritans were evil and only other Jews were their neighbors.

But the point is that the lawyer was wrong about the way the world is. So were the Jewish listeners, and so are we. When Jesus finishes the story, he asks, "Who, in your opinion, was the neighbor?" That's the question that Jesus came to answer in a way that would redefine relationships for everyone in the world. Jesus begins by destroying our notion of "neighbor" so he can later teach us that we are sisters and brothers of each other. But one can't be a sister if one can't even be a neighbor.

Let's try it ourselves. Let us each ask ourselves, "Who is my neighbor?" and translate that to mean, "In times of trouble, whom do I need to help, and how much?" If we ask it that way, we would have to make the circle of neighbors as small as we can, because we all feel poor and we don't have the resources (time, energy, generosity, or money) to help very many people.

But if we invert the question: "Who should help me if I am in trouble?" the answer changes drastically. If I'm in the ditch, I'll take help from anyone. So suddenly my perception changes. That's what Jesus does for the lawyer: He gives him the victim's view. When he changes that, the lawyer radically challenges his unconscious definition of "neighbor."

Religious and civil authorities killed Jesus because of the message of parables like that. Why? Because that kind of thinking ruins social, national, and religious boundaries, and they knew it. It still does. For example, what would happen to our welfare program if one of the cabinet members were on welfare? Or had the spiritual imagination to see the welfare program through the eyes of the woman with small children in the waiting room?

If someone has a vested interest in seeing the world "just the way it is" (according to *their* viewpoint), with all the classes, privileges, and boundaries the way they are (lawyers, the wealthy, the military—depending on what boundaries you have in mind), it is almost impossible to change his mind. That's why Jesus says:

> **I thank thee, Father, Lord of heaven and earth, that thou hast hidden these things from the wise and understanding and revealed to babes. . . .**
>
> **—Luke 10:21**

This saying is often used to praise or condone ignorance, but in the political context of Jesus' time it is best understood as a condemnation of the rigidity of the forces in power. The cleverness of such entrenched, powerful forces prevents them from seeing the radical equality of everyone. California voters recently passed Proposition 187, canonizing their state political boundaries, so that "illegals" not born there are now specifically not entitled to education or health care. But Californians are no worse than people anywhere else: We all have our boundaries that we try to enforce—community, zoning, neighborhood, fiscal, or political boundaries. And parables dissolve these artificial boundaries.

For example. Everybody loves and quotes the parable of the lilies of the field:

> **Take the lilies: they do not spin, they do not weave; but I tell you, Solomon in all his splendor was not arrayed like any one of them. If God clothes in such splendor the grass of the field, which grows today and is thrown on the fire tomorrow, how much more will he provide for you, oh weak in faith.**
>
> **—Luke 12:27–28**

If we take this as advice, it is bad advice. But this is not Luke's little instruction book on how to do career planning. Once again, it is instead Jesus reminding us that conventional wisdom, practical plans for getting ahead, and notions of civic responsibility are all equally ambiguous. To make them into rigid absolutes is a mistake. These concepts are not written in stone. Only God is God—everything else is relative and pales into insignificance. And the bottom line is not the bottom line—that is just an accounting metaphor. Jesus says "Whatever you think about the world, you're wrong."

Which leads directly to the Enneagram.

The Enneagram is a personality typing system that has as its major premise that we are wrong about the way we see the world. Each of the nine types sees the world in a specific way and considers that way to be the total picture. It isn't. Each type is in its own trance, but we are all in trances, like people walking around with a flashlight in a dark room. What we see, we see clearly, but what we don't see is also important—and can hurt us.

Richard Rohr says each of the nine types sees one ninth of the truth. Each of the types is in a kind of trance. The Enneagram personality system asserts that our nine differing worldviews are profound and remain hidden from us, as all trances do. A trance makes our neurotic/sinful actions seem entirely reasonable. Many people, upon finding their types, burst into tears or even become physically ill.

One's Enneagram type is, on one hand, like a nationality. All nationalities are distinct, with good and bad traits depending on circumstance, and with corresponding consequences. That analogy tells us that our Enneagram trance gives us a certain set of characteristics. But nationality is a more benevolent analogy, because our Enneagram trance is about what we hear and won't listen to, see and don't understand. Our "distinctiveness" is our distortion. The 1995 Fall issue of the *Enneagram educator* has a list of crazy thoughts that each type thinks. The Enneagram can indeed be seen as a system that describes nine ways to be crazy, or nine ways to be sinful.

The Enneagram types are often defined by a single adjective. Ones are called "perfectionist," for example. Such a description can be a starting point if one understands that the "perfectionist" drive in the One is metaphoric. But One-ness is not simply a trait, not merely a behavior. It is a complex energy, a repeating strategy for dealing with an impoverished world. The identification of this energy is so difficult that Enneagram leaders sometimes mistype people, disagree with each other, or use different terms to describe the types. An energy can manifest itself in a particular form one day and in another the next.

Recently a knowledgeable Enneagram student told me that Sevens are always, compulsively, on time. But I know an Enneagram teacher who, as a personal policy, will not go to dinner with Sevens because they are always late. The Seven's compulsion to avoid conflict can lead either to being on time to avoid repercussions or to postponing dinner appointments as long as possible with someone they fear may give them grief.

So one cannot easily predict specific behavior just from the type. The behavior may be only a strategy, and the strategy is a response to a world an outsider can't see because that world doesn't really exist! That world may be the world of the person when she was three years old.

The metaphoric energy of the Enneagram comes from trying to integrate a distorted worldview with a corresponding strategy for dealing with that world. The more unhealthy the person is, the more rigid and repetitive that strategy becomes. If a type Four felt sick and wronged at age five and his wailing then got him attention, he may continue that behavior indefinitely. Or the "wailing" may become metaphoric: He may see himself as a misfit, or see everyone else as somehow better than him, "desiring this man's art and that man's scope" as Shakespeare put it (Sonnet 29). Or he may love to pray the Psalms of lamentation in his prayer life. Yet if we simply see the sin of the Four as envy, the flexibility, unpredictability, and the fundamentally polymorphous nature of the energy is missed. Many of the mainstream books—and even more so, the articles popularizing the Enneagram—do a one-page (or one-paragraph) analysis of each type. That's usually a disservice, valid only as a parlor game.

The Enneagram asserts that every person has one chief feature or major distortion and this distortion is called our personality. But our Enneagram flaw is not what we are; it is what we are not. That's a slightly different understanding of personality than usual. Another way of understanding the Enneagram compulsion is to say it is a trance at the level of personality. One may have a political trance—"all liberals are . . ." or "all conservatives are . . ."—but the Enneagram trance is the deepest trance of all.

It is no accident that the traditional seven sins of medieval scholastic philosophy are seven of the nine Enneagram types. Our Enneagram style is a sin, for "sin" is, first of all, a perception of the world, not just the activities that flow from it. That's why faith is so important, as a perception of the world under the benevolent and powerful care of God. The Enneagram, in its description of our sins and its clear understanding of the relationship between perception and action, helps us understand why what we believe has such a powerful influence on what we do. Neitzsche observed that if there is no God, anything is possible. In a world without meaning, "wrong" or "sick" or "evil" behavior is also meaningless. The word *dysfunction* is a skinny word that says our behavior isn't doing what it should be doing —whatever that might be. *Dysfunction* is the kind of word we use when we are at sea about the larger issues of meaning, purpose, and pleasure.

The word *sin* has been trivialized by contemporary usage. People who don't take God seriously tend to use theological language inappropriately: A car becomes Infinity, perfumes claim every sort of sensual taboo, angels are debased hourly, and sin itself is no longer hard currency in moral transactions. Ice cream and candy are "sinfully delicious," things are "sinfully pleasurable." Even the reputable Baltimore Catechism said that for a sin to be worthwhile, the sinner had to give full consent and be in full control of his or her faculties ("free"), and that sin had to be a serious matter.

But even this definition somewhat trivializes sin because it implies that sin is an act that we can commit or not commit as we wish. It also says that we only sin when we are in full control of the situation. It asserts that sin is in direct proportion to freedom. It is no wonder that Catholics felt ashamed for confessing the same sin over and over. If people sin in proportion to the amount of free will they possess, then they should just stop being bad and start being good. But it doesn't work that way.

Paul had a different notion of sin, as does the Enneagram. They both maintain that sin is a power we can't break, a destructive force over which we have little control. And it does us in: The wages (consequences) of sin are death. Paul writes:

> I am carnal, sold under sin. I do not understand my own actions. For I do not do what I want, but I do the very thing I hate. . . . For I know that nothing good dwells within me, that is, in my flesh. I can will what is right, but I cannot do it. For I do not do the good I want, but the evil I do not want is what I do. Now if I do what I do not want, it is no longer I that do it, but sin which dwells within me.
>
> —Romans 7:14, 18

So speak serious students of the Enneagram also. Sin is a destructive force that dwells within us that has us do what we don't want to do. When an Eight walks through life expecting hostility at every turn, the attitude is not a voluntary choice. When a One can see only what is wrong with the world, the viewpoint is painful and is not chosen voluntarily. When a Four can only focus on what is wrong with her, that situation hurts.

So when Jesus said that he came to preach forgiveness of sins, he was taking on the task of breaking the habits of thought and action that keep us from acting in any way except the one that fits our distorted worldview. That's why the New Testament uses the word, *metanoia*, meaning "to change one's mind." Faith is not a body of information; it is a worldview in which God is present, creating a whole universe in which we can nourish ourselves.

Now the approach of Jesus becomes more profound. It might make sense for Jesus to say "Your sins are forgiven," if our sins were just a series of bad acts. But how is Jesus going to forgive a strategy rooted in a distorted worldview? By parables.

Parables don't just announce the forgiveness of sins; they destroy the sinful perspective in their very telling. Parables were intended to convince Jesus' followers that they didn't have to respond the way they always had because the world was different than they had thought. The parables were unraveling devices.

calculated to shatter their rigid, self-protecting habits of thought and action that were so self-destroying.

Perhaps another parable can make this clearer. We have heard it said that we should mend our ways, stop being bad, start being good, and get rid of our faults. Shape up. But Jesus says:

> **The kingdom of heaven may be compared to a man who sowed good seed in his field; but while men were sleeping, his enemy came and sowed weeds among the wheat, and went away. So when the plants came up and bore grain, then the weeds appeared also. And the servants of the householder came and said to him, "Sir, did you not sow good seed in your field? How then has it weeds?" He said to them, "An enemy has done this." The servants said to him, "Then do you want us to go and gather them?" But he said, "No; lest in gathering the weeds you root up the wheat along with them. Let both grow together until the harvest; and at the harvest time I will tell the reapers, 'Gather the weeds first and bind them in bundles to be burned, but gather the wheat into my barn.'"**
>
> **—Matthew 13:24–30**

This is a parable, not advice on how to farm. Kingdom behavior doesn't insist that we get rid of our faults, even our Enneagram faults. Twos will always be proud and Fives avaricious. If someone tries to stop being a need-searching Two, she may dry up some important wells of generosity, too. If a Five stops being detached and observant, he may cease to be the superb writer or scientist that Fives frequently become. If it is not immediately apparent why our gifts are our curse, the Enneagram makes that principle abundantly clear.

At first, Jesus sounds immoral here, allowing people to go on sinning instead of urging them to pull the weeds out of their gardens. Anyone who has been to therapy or has considered the moral dimension of religion seriously knows how urgently and frequently people are admonished to stop doing bad things. The price for moral improvement is a constant elimination of faults and a corresponding cultivation of virtues. Everybody but Jesus seems to know that. People make a living by being critics, therapists, teachers, and writers—all to help people pull out their weeds.

These admonitions and moral urgings—how effective are they? What is our reaction to someone giving us a sermon? How efficacious is nagging? When a parent or teacher or boss says, "I've told you a hundred times . . ."—shouldn't it be apparent that advice given a hundred times simply isn't working?

So Jesus refrains from moralizing or giving advice. Instead he tells us it is more important to accept ourselves than to change. Of course, contemporary therapists would hasten to add that self-acceptance precedes an effective change. It is possible Jesus knew that. More important, knowing that we are acceptable to God makes it a lot easier to accept ourselves. Just talk to a divorced woman who wants to receive the Eucharist and is told she is not worthy. Ask her what it does to her self-esteem to be rejected by the Church in the name of God.

Parables operate differently than instruction books. A parable works by capturing your imagination. It lodges deep in your soul, and when you get ready to make a decision, the parable is there. You've seen it happen lots of times. Someone will do a favor and when thanked, will say, "Oh, well, I was just trying to be a Good Samaritan." Or a wayward son will be called the prodigal (The word *prodigal* has practically been co-opted by this parable of the father and his two sons). Secular aphorisms and proverbs work in much the same way. Businessmen who couldn't thread a needle to save their bottom line say things like "A stitch in time saves nine." Even though they have no experience in sewing, the metaphor is powerful enough to influence their decisions.

We let parables into our life and gradually we live according to their wisdom. Their moral contours become ours—and as that happens, we become free from our compulsions.

No one parable is going to magically untie all the neurotic strings that bind us all at once. Jesus told us in parable form that they wouldn't. He said the kingdom of God is like a mustard seed (Luke 13:19): It starts out small and ends up being truly significant. The Jews listening to this parable were expecting a political and economic triumph from Yahweh, as the Lord had done against the enemies of David and the kings of old. The metaphor of the mustard seed would have contradicted all cultural expectations. The Jews wanted external political intervention, the parable told them divine intervention would be internal and moral, an experience of dynamic inner grace. The mustard seed is a metaphor for patience. Jesus is saying, in a way that will liberate our imagination, "Make small changes in your life." He said the same thing in another parable:

> **To what shall I compare the kingdom of God? It is like leaven which a woman took and hid in three measures of meal, till it was all leavened.**
>
> **—Luke 13:20**

Even the truest believer has a right to be suspicious of the radical conversions featured on certain television programs. To go from being a highly compulsive, stingy, deceptive, avaricious jerk to becoming an enlightened, self-giving, compassionate, self-actualized human being in the space of a single TV show is in direct violation of the laws of creation. And the author of creation is highly unlikely to suspend permanent laws for our temporary convenience. What usually happens—as any priest, minister, or therapist can tell you—is that the Enneagram compulsion is simply redirected. Instead of being totally addicted to drugs or food or sex, the person is now equally rigidly addicted to a narrow range of religious words and behaviors.

So regardless of your Enneagram style and your degree of health, if you want to make some steps toward the light, just remember your development is like a mustard seed. It's true. That's the way the kingdom works.

Ones

VIRTUE IS ITS OWN REWARD

Every Enneagram style is a way of trying to cope with the fact that we have a wrong way of viewing the world. It is equally true that each Enneagram style denotes a bad strategy for trying to win the approval of God, according to our own definition of him or her.

In our secular society, our need and desire to please God goes underground. We are not usually aware of the primitive fear of God that we have. We have a cosmic *malaise*. We are conscious of a vague dissatisfaction with who we are, we are angry with our governments because the world doesn't work right, and we try everything we know to build our own self-esteem and that of our children. But we don't acknowledge our fears that maybe we have something all wrong. We don't know how or if we should be seeking to placate God.

Ones have it all figured out. The way Ones fit best into the world and make it manageable is by being morally correct. If Ones are religious, they become morally correct in line with their religion. If they are not, they become morally correct about politics or music or manners. Whatever they do, they do it right.

The Hebrew Scriptures are a chronicle of God's rejection of our efforts to gain divine approval by doing things right. God keeps redirecting our attention from pleasing Heaven to taking care of each other. But many of us still prefer to curry favor with Heaven.

23

In the beginning, trying to please God took the form of human sacrifice, which was so common at the time Genesis was written that the real achievement of Abraham seems to be not that he was willing to sacrifice his son—which seemed as reasonable to his contemporaries as our sacrificing our young men to war— but that he had the moral fiber *not* to sacrifice Isaac. He abruptly broke with tradition, for sacrifice was the only way his culture knew to make peace on earth with God.

The Mosaic Law was many good things, but one of the reasons the Jews loved the Law so thoroughly was that they believed if they followed the Law, they would be pleasing to God. The Law was the supreme gift of Yahweh, the sign of the covenant between the Lord and his People. The Law was the will of God. Those who followed it knew they were right. A One's paradise.

Ones tend to appreciate law: Jewish law, natural law, city ordinances, traffic laws, any laws. Laws help Ones carry out their conviction that life is a theater for moral heroism. Life is a moral struggle, or it is pointless.

When healthy, their moral acuity makes Ones fair, balanced, and responsible. They make wonderful judges, police, and civic leaders. They exercise admirable moral courage and will fight for what is right just because it is right; they are not swayed by self-interest or outside pressure. Whether or not you agree with John Paul II, who is a One, you have to admit he says what he thinks is right regardless of who thinks he's wrong. Ones are not swayed by popular opinion.

Healthy Ones display a sense of humor, frequently pleasantly self-deprecating. When healthy, they develop a profound compassion for the unfortunate. They often champion the cause of the underdog (Ralph Nader, taking on the automotive industry, and Hillary Clinton, in her health care crusade, are both Ones).

Ones can be unusually hard workers needing little or no supervision. When healthy, they have a moral equivalent of perfect pitch for what is correct. Their judgment is uncommonly sound. They often become music or literary critics—even if they can't create something, they know what's right.

The Pharisees in the New Testament display strong One energies. So when Jesus doesn't obey the law, they are furious, wallowing in prolonged moral outrage. The two parables which follow are both addressed to Ones:

> On a Sabbath, while he was going through the grain-fields, his disciples plucked and ate some ears of grain, rubbing them in their hands. But some of the Pharisees said, "Why are you doing what is not lawful to do on the Sabbath?" And Jesus answered, "Have you not read what David did when he was hungry, he and those who were with him: how he entered the house of God, and took and ate the bread of the Presence, which it is not lawful for any but the priests to eat, and also gave it to those with him?" And he said to them, "The Son of Man is lord of the Sabbath."
>
> —Luke 6:1–5

Only the healthiest Ones can break a law in the light of a higher law. Jesus deliberately broke the law. He could have gotten food elsewhere; he didn't have to eat that grain. Even though Jesus used legal precedent to justify himself, he wanted to make a point: Human need is more important than ritual law. If Ones can focus their moral energy on human need and away from legal abstraction or social propriety, they make real spiritual progress. No sooner does Jesus break one law than he tries it again:

> On another Sabbath, when he entered the synagogue and taught, a man was there whose right hand was withered. And the scribes and the Pharisees watched him, to see whether he would heal on the Sabbath, so that they might find an accusation against him. But he knew their thoughts, and he said to the man who had the withered hand, "Come and stand here." And he rose and stood there. And Jesus said to them, "I ask you, is it lawful on the Sabbath to do good or to do harm, to save life or to destroy it?" And he looked around on them all, and said to him, "Stretch out your hand." And he did so, and his hand was restored. But they were filled with fury and discussed with one another what they might do to Jesus.
>
> —Luke 6:6–11

Several subtleties pertain to the One energy. Notice that Jesus asks them "Is it lawful to do good?" He addressed their strong suit, moral perspicacity, and used it against them. He knew their moral fervor; he knew they would know he was right. By making them choose between goodness and the law, he pitted their two absolutes against each other, putting them in a double bind with their One energy. These two stories are fine examples of an overused energy becoming too focused. Their moral preoccupation had shifted from what is right in one's heart to what is legal—what is right by the book.

But they still have this moral energy, so they turn it against him, always a concern for Ones. Entranced Ones become punitive. Here they are furious.

At this point Jesus apparently gives up on them. The next verse continues:

In these days he went out into the hills to pray; and all night he continued in prayer to God. And when it was day, he called his disciples, and chose from them twelve, whom he named apostles.

—Luke 6:12–13

The Pharisees' entranced One-based tradition is bankrupt, so Jesus starts over with the new twelve apostles to replace the twelve tribes of Israel.

When Paul announced to the followers of Jesus that the Law was no longer binding, he frightened them. If they didn't follow the Law, how could they be sure of being pleasing to God? How would they know they were good people?

Paul remained adamant:

Foolish Galatians! . . . Let me ask you only this: Did you receive the Spirit by works of the law or by hearing with faith? Are you so foolish? Having begun with the Spirit, are you now ending with the flesh?

—Galatians 3:1–3

All of the letters to Galatians and Romans wrestle with the necessity of moral struggle and the absolute gratuity of the grace of salvation. It's as though first God said we didn't have to offer human sacrifice, then we didn't have to offer any sacrifice and finally he revealed that he loved us regardless of what we did. Any One is apt to see that God is getting soft. It is beyond the scope of my work to analyze the epistles to Romans and Galatians here, but for a One it would be a spiritual adventure to read them both as being addressed to the righteous energy of law-abiding Ones.

St. Paul was a One, and his epistles to the Galatians and the Romans are a detailed examination of a major problem for all of the Enneagram types, but for Ones in a specifically intense way. When Ones, individually or collectively, become unhealthy, they use morality as a club. They become moral vigilantes, fault-seeking missiles that seek and destroy. Ones are often quite uncomfortable within themselves, because what they do unto others, they do unto themselves. They have within themselves a stern and scolding voice that repeatedly accuses them of less than perfection. They can try harder until they break.

Their sin is anger. Their anger doesn't flare up and abuse people. It is the cold controlled disapproval of what others—and they themselves—do and, ultimately, of what they are. They have a special problem—they deny the anger because anger is a sin (and they don't do bad things). So they both are filled with and in denial of anger.

WHAT ONES WANT

Ones really want peace. Not at any price, though; they want what is described in the Hebrew Scriptures as *shalom*. *Shalom* is the full dynamic life in harmony with God and the universe. Some Enneagram teachers say Ones want serenity, but that has to be understood as the serenity of a happy, energetic, buzzing family, not the serenity of a pool of water in which nothing moves. Ones try to achieve this dynamic equilibrium through moral effort. They have a vision of how it ought to be and this vision requires Herculean effort, especially inner exertion, the kind of energy it takes to maintain integrity in spite of attractive contrary options.

WHAT THEY SETTLE FOR

They settle for order. When entranced, they shrink their world until it is small enough to make it orderly. They become obsessed with control, even control over the inner feelings and desires of others. Ones are addicted to anger, a specific anger in the service of moral order. As they grow healthier, they accept more and more of (by their standards, imperfect) reality. As they grow more entranced, they fix on smaller and smaller concerns. The Pharisaic tradition acted it out on a grand scale. They created what was called a hedge. To make sure the Ten Commandments were obeyed, they made some smaller stricter laws around them to protect people from accidentally breaking the Big Ten. Then those smaller laws became absolute, and they made even more detailed laws to protect the protecting laws. This hedge-building process kept on for centuries, until it was understood at the time of Jesus that nobody could keep all the laws.

It's clear that a moral trance can make one feel unloved by God. Ones are convinced that to be a good person (or to please God) is difficult. Scott Peck's moralistic classic *The Road Less Traveled*, begins dramatically with the One's manifesto: "Life is difficult."

Ones habitually compare what is to what should be. It becomes clear why they love the Law. The Law enables them not only to be sure what they are doing is right, but it has the interesting side effect of being able to compare my behavior with others and see what they are doing right, or, juicily, what they are doing wrong. When in their trance, Ones love objective external standards, and what better validation is there than Divine Law?

Validation is not accidental. Ones are critical of everything and everybody, but the real pain of the One is her own self-criticism. The artist who draws those cartoons with little conscience-voices and devil-voices looking over people's shoulders understands Ones perfectly. Ones are self-critical to a fault. They hurt themselves with self-criticism, so it is a relief when they have an objective, unchallenged, clear authoritative law. Then they know they are right. It is such a relief to tell the little voice on their shoulders that they have obeyed the law perfectly. It's like getting an "A" from their pickiest teacher.

So when Jesus comes along and announces that by *faith* we fulfill the Law, Ones are thrown into turmoil: "How can I tell? Who can tell me if I have faith or not?" Paul's letters to the Galatians and Romans are so powerful and thorough because they were Paul's own working-out of that question. And it is not accidental that Martin Luther, similarly obsessed with being justified, was a One.

But don't try to explain all of Pauline theology or Luther's treatises on grace by reducing their authors to Enneagram types. All their Enneagram type did was make them extra sensitive to certain areas of revelation. Ones are sensitive to the delicate relationship between moral effort and freely given grace.

Ones are convinced that the world and each one of us is flawed. And further, our flaw needs to be and can be corrected. They are angry about that. They are angry that reality is not the way it should be. They resent the moral inadequacy of things in general. So they become skilled at noticing what is wrong. Then they employ the anger (which is energy to bring about change) to make things better so that reality will be more lovable—lovable by them and, more importantly, by God. Criticism is for "their own good." It is an act of love, saving them from themselves. If we love someone, we don't let them make mistakes.

So imagine how much a One needs to hear this parable:

What is your thought on this: A man owns a hundred sheep and one of them wanders away; will he not leave the ninety-nine out on the hills and go in search of the stray? If he succeeds in finding it, believe me he is happier about this one than about the ninety-nine that did not wander away. Just so, it is no part of your heavenly Father's plan that a single one of these little ones shall ever come to grief.

—Matthew 18:12–14

What do you think? If a man has a hundred sheep, and one of them has gone astray, does he not leave the ninety-nine on the hills and go in search of the one that went astray? And if he finds it, truly, I say to you, he rejoices over it more than over the ninety-nine that never went

astray. So it is not the will of my Father, who is in heaven, that one of these little ones should perish.

—Luke 15:3–7

The Ones' first temptation, in understanding this parable, is to make it into a new moral command. They say, "Oh, repentance is of greater spiritual value than fidelity to moral behavior." Then they develop this theme. In Matthew, Jesus doesn't mention repentance. But Luke does. The repentance theme is a more than likely Lucan addition and interpretation of the original parable. It is important, but notice the moralizing that creeps into this version.

The simple message of the parable is that when we understand the kingdom, the distinction between good and bad people is obliterated. God loves bad people, too. Ones don't emotionally appreciate this. But notice: Luke positions this parable as a response to the Pharisees' objection to Jesus eating with sinners:

And the Pharisees and the scribes murmured, saying, "This man receives sinners and eats with them."

—Luke 15:2

The Pharisees' objection interprets the parable for us by raising the objection to which this parable is the response. Jesus came to make friends with, be intimate with, and offer the kingdom of God to sinners. Ones need to notice that the Law actually *creates* sinners, in Paul's sense, because it divides people into those who obey and those who don't. When Jesus has forgiveness of sin as his central message, he dissolves the boundaries between good guys and bad. The Pharisees never forgot or forgave that. Nor does the entranced One.

So all the effort of the One to make reality conform to their standards is superfluous and frequently counterproductive. God loves reality, including us, the way it is and the way we are. And God loves the One *before* any effort.

This is contrary to what is preached from most pulpits. The usual understanding in the pew is that good people go to heaven, bad people to hell, and most of us are pretty clear who the good and bad people are—that's the implicit and sometimes the explicit message in most sermons. That message is certainly the means of social control by politicians, our legal system, and the business world. Jesus' message comes from a vision that flatly contradicts the customary social vision to which the entranced One says, "Amen."

This parable is not good advice. It's not advice at all. It is not instruction on how to be a shepherd. The single meaning of the parable is that though we may still consider ourselves lost, God is relentlessly offering us love. Ones are energetically and angrily seeking what they already have—love and harmony with God.

The parable goes beyond advice into mystery and creates a fruitful tension within us. We are the object of an intense search by the creative force of the universe, our Father. This search for us is not dependent on our puny moral effort. A universal force that can create mountains of gas six trillion miles high in outer space is not apt to be impressed by one's moral exertion. The Good Shepherd is unceasingly looking for us; we are constantly being offered love, even if—or perhaps especially when—we are lost. Jesus offered the parable as a refutation of our arbitrary division of humanity into those who are sinners and those who aren't, those God loves and those he doesn't. The situation described transcends moral categories, consistent with Jesus' admonition not to judge.

The pitfall of the law is that it creates insiders and outsiders, good and bad people, sacred and profane, kosher and unclean, Jew and Gentile. But we know how much genetic make-up, environmental influence, and apparently simple luck have to do with our status in life. One person robs a bank and gets caught, beginning a life cycle of jail, parole, job difficulties, crime, jail, and the like. Another robs the bank, doesn't get caught, decides against a life of crime (now that he's well off), and becomes a civic pillar. Each of us knows certain twists in our own path that make us catch our breath. What appears to be an objective standard simply isn't. The usual rules don't apply when you're hungry, frightened, abused, or otherwise "lost."

Jesus came preaching the forgiveness of sins. This was not a conditional forgiveness. It was to tell us that our God does not appreciate human sacrifice, doesn't need careful extensive legal frameworks, does not distinguish between clean and unclean animals or clean or unclean people. Ultimately the brotherhood and sisterhood of all people, the fatherhood of God, and the forgiveness of sins are all seen as only one reality seen from different points of view.

Ones, considering moral heroism their ticket to peace on earth and acceptance by God, often have a hard time with this doctrine and this parable. So of course, it is meant for them.

Ones try too hard, morally. When people try too hard, we feel sorry for them at first, but often our feelings turn to frustration and even anger. And within the One strategy, that's what happens within themselves. They try so hard to be good, but they see mainly their shortcomings because they judge themselves against higher and higher standards and so become angry at themselves. It is hard for them to acknowledge they are lost and the Good Shepherd is looking for them, too. The authority of Scripture can be helpful; it is an objective standard that undoes their need for objective standards.

The example of Jesus is helpful. He couldn't and wouldn't meet the standards of the Pharisees. They criticized everything he did: eating grain on the Sabbath, healing people, interpreting the Scriptures, eating with sinners, associating with women of ill repute—a list long enough to make any One pause for reflection.

Ones attempt an impossible task. It isn't until they give up the job of making themselves pleasing to God through their efforts that they make any progress either in emotional or spiritual development. Jesus tells the following parable:

> He also told this parable to some who trusted in themselves that they were righteous and despised others: "Two men went up into the temple to pray, one a Pharisee and the other a tax collector. The Pharisee stood and prayed thus with himself, 'God, I thank thee that I am not like other men, extortioners, unjust, adulterers, or even like this tax collector. I fast twice a week, I give tithes of all that I get.' But the tax collector, standing far off, would not even lift up his eyes to heaven, but beat his breast, saying, 'God, be merciful to me a sinner!' I tell you, this

man went down to his house justified rather than the
other; for every one who exalts himself will be humbled,
but he who humbles himself will be exalted."

—Luke 18:9–14

The One energy is laid bare here in several ways. In some traditions, type One is called the comparing mind. Her particular
skew is comparing reality to what ought to be, but it soon
spills over into comparing herself with others and comparing
her behavior with the requirements of the objective law. The
Pharisee falls directly into this trap, comparing himself with
the law and the tax collector (who by legal definition was a
sinner in Palestine at this time). Once we start with the
premise that the other person is a sinner, we can be fairly sure
of looking good.

Religious people are expected to be morally good. Jesus
warned his disciples that their justice had to exceed that of the
Pharisees. So he isn't against good behavior. But why does a public sinner receive approval? What did he do?

He acknowledged reality. He admitted his faults. Perhaps
the Enneagram's finest contribution is helping us admit our
main fault. No small achievement. Our Enneagram trance is our
adaptation to an unreal remembered world in which we focus on
a few inner realities (in this case the feeling of intense moral
summons) and consider them the whole world. God, mental
health, and true spirituality all demand a grounding in reality.

But how does Jesus get his listeners to acknowledge reality?
Symbolic language. Therapists, preachers, and various teachers
try to get us to acknowledge reality. It is such a fine starting point
for development. Jesus uses parable and paradox that destroy our
personal and cultural expectations. We've heard his words so
many times we think we understand this parable. But our understanding is usually that bragging will get us nowhere—humility is
the virtue we should seek. But Jesus is not prioritizing virtues. He
is establishing our morality at a deeper level. He is saying that our
systematic project of trying to please God is offensive. A baby
doesn't try to delight parents. Its existence does that. Ever notice
how we are irritated when someone "tries too hard?" Why?

Because it is unreal and manipulative. Neither God nor people will love in response to manipulation.

This would be a lot harder to understand if it weren't for Ireland, Bosnia, Palestine, and the various other countries who are waging war in the name of God. The desire to capture God, to assume or prove that God is "on our side" is subtle, pervasive, and corrupting. (This is not a book on how to please God, it is a description of the wrong ways we make the effort.) Ultimately when something is full of grace, it is and looks effortless.

As soon as the Pharisee holds up his behavior as earning the pleasure of God, he is lost. And the example of the Pharisee trying to hoist himself up morally warns the reader that any attempt to set up a formula for guaranteeing grace will be folly.

The radical moral humility required is only gained when we stop trying. We have to do good things—if only to make money, please one's parents, and stay out of jail—but those good things do not win love. Only love wins love.

Obtaining the grace of God is like trying to make the sun rise. Just because it comes up doesn't entitle us to crow in triumph. A certain alertness is praiseworthy, but it is emotionally so important for personal growth to acknowledge that what we accomplish is largely dependent on forces outside us.

Ones can often display a trait that illustrates this. They tend to prefer to be appreciated for the work they do rather than their attractiveness. They can be overlooked for promotion or recognition because of a certain self-righteousness and they are furious because by the criteria "that everyone is supposed to use," they were the best qualified. It is on earth as it is in heaven. People are not loved because of their rectitude. Something else outranks it.

So Jesus tells the story of the Pharisee, which makes the moral task impossible and counterproductive. As a One tries to live this story, he can gradually let go of the impossible task. When he does, he softens, develops a sense of humor and gratitude.

The One's addiction to perfection shrinks her world. The entranced One is virtuous within a carefully circumscribed set of rules. Jesus was always scolding the Pharisees for overlooking the bigger picture, what he called "the weightier matters of the law" (Matthew 23:23). When we try to have a perfect lawn, we make it small. We can't have a perfect twelve-acre manicured lawn. Ones often report getting angry at something and then furiously cleaning their room or vacuuming. They are making one part of the world—a manageable part—perfect. When we do that with laws, we get fussier and fussier about smaller and smaller things at the expense of reality and at the expense of the weightier matters.

If a One becomes concerned about social justice or ecological reform or racial equality, the moral task is so great she can't feel righteous. She hasn't succeeded. As soon as we are sure we are righteous, we automatically create God into our image and likeness: Remember the One compares what is to what ought to be. And Yahweh gave his name as "I AM." God is who IS, and when we compare God to what ought to be, we shrivel Ultimate Reality to fit our moral categories. We become legalists.

With legalism comes a grinding effort. The word grace has harmonics of playfulness, effortlessness, and smoothness. I think the words of Jesus apply particularly to Ones:

Come to me, all who labor and are heavy laden, and I will give you rest.
—Matthew 11:29

A pseudo morality, perfectionism, is the enemy of true morality. That's what is meant when Jesus says:

Think not that I have come to abolish the law and the prophets; I have come not abolish them but to fulfill them. . . . Whoever then relaxes one of the least of these commandments and teaches men so, shall be called least in the kingdom of heaven; but he who does them and teaches them shall be called great in the kingdom of heaven. For I tell you unless your righteousness exceeds that of the scribes and Pharisees, you will never enter the kingdom of heaven.
—Matthew 5:17, 19–20

The paradox of the law being binding *and* inadequate is a source of energy for the spirituality for the One. Their temptation is to stop at binding and call it the whole picture. The big picture for Jesus started with forgiveness, something neither the law nor a legalist can offer. In Matthew 18:21, Jesus tells Peter to forgive his brother seventy times seven, which in effect is as often as he sins. If Ones can learn to forgive themselves and others, they develop the compassion necessary for real spiritual development. Ones might notice that in Jesus' prayer, the Our Father, no moral effort is required except at the end, when we promise to forgive others as we wish to be forgiven. All the rest is up to God.

What Can Ones Do?

1) Develop your sense of humor. It reliably measures your health and spirituality.

2) Treat yourself to aesthetic pleasures. Appreciating a thing's beauty breaks your habit of comparing it to something else. Beautiful religious art and music can help you see God as beautiful as well as moral. That can soften excessive moral focus.

3) Prayer of gratitude helps. It's hard to be simultaneously critical and grateful.

There are many other therapeutic techniques; I select only a few that relate directly to biblical tradition.

TWOS

LOVE'S LABOR INVESTED

Twos are among the most personal of the styles. Regardless of what task they may be doing, they tend to focus primarily on relationships. Healthy Twos may seem the most loving and lovable people in your experience. It's a delight to receive a gift from a Two because she tends to know what you want more keenly than you yourself do. Regardless of the price range, she seldom errs.

And Twos are very adaptable. If you need counsel, the Two is right there. But if you need clerical help, your garden tilled, your car fixed, or your income tax filed, a talented Two will again be your best bet. Twos focus on what you need, with an inner conviction that regardless of what you need, they can help. St. Thomas defined charity as "giving of oneself," and Twos are only too happy to oblige.

But obliging is tricky. It has a double meaning. It means to give to someone, but also to put that person in your debt, to "obligate" them in return. St. Vincent de Paul told his brothers that "the poor must forgive us our charity," cautioning them not to expect gratitude, because not only is it better to give than to receive, but because receiving can be a humiliating—or at least an irritating—experience. Receivers are often obligated to assume that the giver is superior. Twos can easily make the same emotional mistake.

The Enneagram tradition describes the chief feature of the Two as pride, specifically the pride of being able to give without needing anyone to give anything to him. Not acknowledging one's needs is an emotionally arrogant position, so it is called pride, but this differs from the scholastic tradition, wherein pride is the origin and worst of all sins, because pride was, in the Genesis account, trying to be like God.

> **Your eyes will be opened, and you will be like God, knowing good and evil.**
>
> **—Genesis 3:5**

A Two doesn't acknowledge her needs on a conscious level. On a conscious level, she constantly tries to meet the needs of others. But she isn't aware that this is an emotional investment precisely in order to have her own deep (unacknowledged) emotional needs met. The level of depth of trance in the Two is measured quite clearly by how oblivious she is to her own needs. People who have trouble relating to Twos often describe them as needy, but a more accurate description would be "needy and not acknowledging those needs."

A Two often feels "sticky" to others because he demands symbolic fulfillment of his needs ("You never call me"), all the while protesting that his only interest is in meeting another's needs ("If you'd call, I'd be able to do whatever for you"). The message is garbled: "I want this relationship with you because you need it."

Being numb to our own needs is perilous. What we don't get up front, we tend to get out back. So the unhealthy Two keeps an accountant's eye on whether or not she is given as well and as much as she gives. And she may demand reciprocity at rather awkward times. Unhealthy Twos don't really give; they invest. Like all investments, paybacks include interest.

The Twos' adaptability can mutate into confusion about who they are. They're willing to be what other people want, but when someone needs them to be who they really are, Twos draw a blank. They can often live through someone else, in orbit around someone powerful, or for someone else, as in the case of codependency. In clinical terms, they have boundary problems.

WHAT TWOS WANT

Twos want to be loved for their true inner selves. All their attention, their flattery, and some of their manipulation is an attempt to get others to love them for who they are. Twos' lives are about love, and they spend most of their waking hours in search of love. They may not really believe that unconditional love is possible, but that is the central engine of all their activity. Their searching activity is doomed, of course, because love that is earned is, by definition, conditional on what they did to earn it. They succeed by giving up, typical of the paradoxes of Jesus. Often giving up on earning love is the final phase of a spiritual movement for a Two.

WHAT THEY SETTLE FOR

They settle for appreciation. Their background is often one in which they took care of their caretakers in one way or another, either physically or emotionally. So they look for love by taking care of the needs of whomever they love. The painful knot in this transaction is that the Twos' assumption is that people will love them if they take care of them. The negative flip is also true. People won't love them if they don't take care of them. The sin of pride is inflation, and it is appreciation that inflates the Two.

Appreciation falls short of love, however. Imagine the person of your dreams in an intimate moment when you are longing for commitment or affection, saying instead, in pleasant but careful tones, how much he or she *appreciates* all you have done. That doesn't quite make it.

The ill-structured dynamic of the Two trance goes as follows: She begins with a distorted view of reality: people will only love her if she takes care of them and their needs. She gives away that precious self-esteem that says "I'm lovable just as I am." (Watch a cherished child expect to be loved utterly for just smiling.) Then, after having given away their right to unconditional love, they spend all their energy trying to obtain it. And of course they can never get enough conditional love because a chasm exists between conditional love and unconditional love. No amount of conditional (gratitude-based) love adds up to unconditional love.

Chapter 14 of Luke's Gospel records several meal parables that address issues of Twos. The first issue is one of boundaries and love. Twos often have boundary confusion. That means that they invade others' space and time and let others invade theirs inappropriately. Boundaries create identity. If the identity is clear, then one can be loved for one's real self, one's real identity. Without boundaries, there is no identity and no authentic love.

In the Middle Eastern culture of the time of Jesus, one asserted and created identity and boundaries through table fellowship. When Jesus ate with sinners, everyone knew he was challenging the social rules and breaking boundaries. When he ate with sinners, he cast his lot with them. *Sinner* was a technical term meaning someone who did not obey the Jewish laws, someone outside the Jewish community, on the other side of the boundaries, like terrorists today (or communists in the United States, until recently).

The outrage over Jesus' eating habits is hard for us to grasp. But the dietary laws of the Old Testament—so thorough, so detailed, so serious as to cause or destroy identity—were the means of social and personal construction. When we say "you are what you eat," we refer to nutrition. They could use the same phrase with religious and moral significance. Dietary habits were a real measure of Jewish fidelity.

To this day, the orthodoxy of Jews is measured significantly by their adherence to dietary guidelines. *Kosher* means a way of preparing food, but its significance has spread until the word means "that which is right to do." *Kosher* equals moral—and, by extension, religious—identity.

So, knowing full well the crucial importance of table ranking, Jesus tells the following parable (Remember, a parable is not a nice story. It is a story that unravels cultural and spiritual expectations, identity, and principles):

Now he told a parable to those who were invited, when he marked how they chose the places of honor, saying to them, "When you are invited by any one to a marriage feast, do not sit down in a place of honor, lest a more

eminent man than you be invited by him; and he who invited you both will come and say to you, 'Give place to this man,' and then you will begin with shame to take the lowest place. But when you are invited, go and sit in the lowest place, so that when your host comes, he may say to you, 'Friend, go up higher'; then you will be honored in the presence of all who sit at table with you. For every one who exalts himself will be humbled, and he who humbles himself will be exalted."

—Luke 14:7–11

Jesus is not giving good advice here on how to get a higher place at the table, with corresponding social approbation. His parables are about the principles of the kingdom of God. And this one is no exception.

This parable addresses the Two's boundary and identity concerns. The Jews set boundaries between those with whom they would eat and those with whom they wouldn't eat. That put them in control of the purity of the nation as a whole. It also worked in smaller units, separating good and bad guys. So if a certain pride and self-inflation is the problem, careful eating habits is a solution. Eating sets up social and emotional distinctions that bring status and esteem. Someone's position at the table confers the longed-for identity and status.

But watch how the parable dissolves the distinctions. Want to get spiritually dizzy? Try this. You want to be exalted, so you humble yourself to get exalted. But since humbling yourself is just a technique to help get a higher status, to get exalted, by humbling yourself, you're really trying to exalt yourself. Doesn't quite work, does it?

Or reverse it. You want to be humble. How are you going to become humble? By exalting yourself, of course. So if you want to become humble, go around bragging and people will think less of you and you'll be humble. But among the humble people you know and admire, how many of them bragged their way to virtue? Or try to pick an example from the Scriptures or the lives of the saints—find someone who exalted herself to acquire the virtue of humility. Can you find one?

Nevertheless, some people try a form of this. Think of how many times you've heard people who do good work say, as they show it to you, "Oh, I know it's not very good. I really can't draw [or paint, or sing, or throw—whatever]." And you know full well they want you to praise them. And you usually resent it. You reluctantly praise them or withhold your praise altogether, for you know they are playing a game.

People who have taken this parable literally tend to play the game. When it fails, they make a big deal out of saying that humility is just "being honest"—which would come as a surpise to Jesus, who never intended us to take his parable literally.

The point is: Parables are not techniques. Don't do what they *say*. Don't go around bragging or groveling. That doesn't work. Both extremes are subtle forms of spiritual investment, always a trap for the Two.

So if the parable is not good advice, not a technique for spiritual advancement, why is it there? And why doesn't Jesus just "tell it like it is"?

The parable addresses the problem of self-esteem and the social boundaries that support it and points out that there is a Catch-22 involved. "Catch-22" is a wonderful phrase we have now to describe a problem that cannot be solved on the level on which it is presented. What Jesus does is point out that the problem of self-esteem (and in the culture of the New Testament, social honor) cannot be solved on the level on which it is presented, namely, having someone give or take it from you. The parable shows us that our rank in the kingdom of God can't be acquired by taking it. Neither can it be garnered by *not* taking it (by pretending we aren't taking it, by humbling ourselves). Jesus forces us to give up. At the moment we give up, we're ready for the intervention of grace, or as the physicist Ilya Prigogene puts it, an "escape to a higher order."

Jesus' parables are usually about the nature of the kingdom of God. So they are unintelligible without prayer. And they assume, moment by moment, a relationship to God that makes a serious difference in everything we do.

We can't exalt ourselves in God's opinion, which is what Jesus is indicating. He is promoting "kingdom behavior."

Neither can we humble ourselves in God's opinion. The object of the game is not to try to change our status with God; it is to be grateful for our status with God.

This illustrates the Two's sin of pride. Pride is not, in the eyes of God or in the experience of the Two, claiming his value or identity. It is trying to get others to give it to him. What we have from others is extrinsic, always remaining outside us and subject to loss at any time. What we have from God is within us and can't be taken. Pride looks for a place at the emotional and spiritual table by being assigned there by someone other than God. Unhealthy Twos try to earn love by meeting others' needs instead of their own and telling themselves that they have no needs.

This is simply not true. That's why it is the sin of pride, rather than the legitimate pride everyone takes in gifts and accomplishments. Twos need a grounding in their relationship with God. Prayer is not something we do for a while for any one of a dozen motives. It is an expression of our radical neediness and equally radical gratitude for everything we are and have. When we express this, and when this permeates our understanding then we know and love who we are. In the case of Twos, when they give up jostling for position at the table, their Father assigns them a place and they rejoice in it. This frees them from the evaluations and responses of others, and from their dependence and their need to manipulate.

So the parable taunts us until it breaks our mind-set. When we try to live it on a literal level, we see how convoluted our thinking becomes; if we try to reduce the parable to a technique for achieving our place at the table of the Lord, our real place in life, it just doesn't work.

I talked to one of my students who understood this intuitively. He was "cool" and he knew it. His grades were good, his body strong, he had style, grace, and charm. Little girls (he was eleven) came to watch him play ball, weaker boys followed him, glad of tag-along privileges. So after class one day, I asked him about one of the kids who was having trouble, "Why isn't Jimmy cool?" He answered, without hesitation, "Because he tries too hard to be." I knew he was right and was impressed that he was, but I decided to push it. "Well, how is he going to become cool if he doesn't try?" He said he didn't know, but he knew that if you weren't cool, you couldn't make yourself cool. So I asked him, "Well, how do you get be cool?" He answered coolly, "You don't have to try, you just are."

Pretty good theology of grace for an eleven-year-old. Jesus is telling us something similar: Twos need to assimilate in prayer the ability to relax. They don't have to keep meeting people's needs; they don't have to ingratiate themselves. Their Father, who knows what those needs are, will take care of those needs.

Don't misunderstand. We must meet the needs of others: The world would be an awful place if we didn't. We simply shouldn't think we have earned love by doing it. Meeting others' needs is an art, and if the impulse arises out of our own neediness, we will get it all wrong.

The parable emphasizes that one does things out of a sense of gratitude for all that we have been given. It is not investment; it is saying thanks. This goes entirely against the cultural expectations of then and now. The common-sense understanding of New Testament people raised on the Law was that if people kept the Law, they would be righteous in the eyes of God. The same notion is preached on most Sundays—we should be good in order to get to heaven. That's the dangerous position Twos really assimilate on an emotional level. That's also the position condemned by Paul all through the epistles to the Galatians and Romans. Paul's condemnation of living by the Law isn't merely of historical interest; it is rooted in a profound understanding of the structural damage it does to our emotional life, as is the parable's.

The problem called the sin of pride is in not acknowledging neediness—especially our need of God. Keeping the Law is a subtle way of getting along without God, without the radical opening to the void within us. The words we use are "God's Law," but the emotional reality is our self-justification without admitting our tumultous creaturehood.

Trying to deal with Jesus' parables without an emotionally rich, nuanced, and constant reference to reliance on God empties them of their deep meaning. The assumption behind this parable is that when we give up trying to figure out how to be loved, we will entrust the whole enterprise to our Father. But unless we pray to God as intimate and relational, the parables are just frustrating. One can't take Jesus' parables out of the context of the Gospels. Jesus said he only did what he saw the Father doing. The parables make visible the dynamics of the life of grace that Jesus lived.

Our Enneagram style is what we do when we don't watch what our Father is doing, when we are not aware of the full richness of reality created by God for our happiness. Our Enneagram style is a reactive strategy to a world we perceive as impoverished because that has been our early or repeated experience. The kingdom vision Jesus promotes is one of richness, of paradise and abundance.

I love to watch skilled therapists. They point out that the compulsive energy we customarily ride is being frustrated by "circumstance." Often we hear people who are trying to make spiritual sense of their lives say things like, "It's like the universe was trying to tell me something." Our Enneagram strategy hits walls, betraying us and frustrating us. It's bound to, because our Enneagram strategy is based on a partial view of the world. But we can only give it up if we trust that God will do something better in our lives.

The next parable in Luke is addressed to another expression of the Two compulsion:

> He said also to the man who had invited him, "When you give a dinner or a banquet, do not invite your friends or your brothers or your kinsmen or rich neighbors, lest they also invite you in return, and you be repaid. But when you give a feast, invite the poor, the maimed, the lame, the blind, and you will be blessed, because they cannot repay you. You will be repaid at the resurrection of the just." When one of those who sat at table with him heard this, he said to him, "Blessed is he who shall eat bread in the kingdom of God."
>
> **—Luke 14:12–15**

Just the advice a Two wants to hear! Don't do anything that will prompt people to love you back. Twos can feel this parable as a frontal attack.

If one takes this literally, then Christian behavior would be to eat only with those people who are not your friends. Imagine your joy at being invited! Besides, if you did need a meal, you couldn't go to eat with your friends. Is this going to work?

There is the spirituality mentioned earlier called *agere contra,* in Latin (usually blamed on the Jesuits, but practiced widely by many non-Jesuits without the benefit of the Latin tag). It is shorthand for the opinion that the way you approach a spiritual or moral problem is by doing the opposite. If you are lazy, the way you solve that problem is by working hard. If you are frightened, do brave things. If you are shy, go meet people. In brief, when in doubt, do what you don't want to do. This approach is very appealing to people who think they have a lot of will power, or have low self-esteem and think that whatever they want is wrong. You've probably been exposed to this opinion. People have had splendid success with this in dealing with weight problems. If you weigh too much, just stop eating so much. If you do this, you are assured of losing weight.

This has worked for you and all your friends hasn't it? If it hasn't, then what you need is more will power. Just do it. (If you really *don't* want to, of course.)

This is a muscular piety. To go around doing all the things you don't want to takes a lot of self-discipline and moral strength. It is the equivalent of the political "pulling yourself up by your bootstraps." The young, the privileged, the healthy, and wealthy tend to favor this spirituality. The Church condemned this opinion as heresy in the third century. It's called Pelagianism and this heresy says that you can attain to the kingdom of God by just doing what is right. This heresy says that if you will be good, you will go to heaven. It is still being preached from many pulpits today, but it is heresy and it is psychologically destructive.

If you could reach heaven or enter the kingdom of God by your own moral muscle, you wouldn't need the gospel or a redeemer. The law would work fine. The message of the Pelagian is that the way to solve your problems, or deal with your Enneagram style, is simply to stop being bad and start being good. In the case of a Two, just stop being nice to friends and inviting them over. Instead, invite the lame and blind and beggars and then you won't be manipulating your friends. Of course, you won't be eating with them either.

A recipe for disaster.

Jesus is not giving advice on how to run your social calendar. If you take this literally, you will be doing all the things I described above.

So what is he saying to the Two? Keep in mind, there is a third party—the Father. When we give to those who can't give back, we give praise and thanks to our Father. We believe full well that whatever we do to the poor, our Father who sees in secret, will give us back. It is not a selfless act for the person of faith. Selflessness is more than humans can pull off and healthy people know that. Unhealthy Twos have selflessness as their primary trap. People doing social ministry often talk about the essential need for a healthy prayer life to avoid burnout. Our individual resources are not enough to meet the needs of everyone. Healthy Twos need to let that truth sink in. The way to help is in conscious awareness of what God does first.

If we do any act as an investment to get God to give us more, we are essentially wrong. All that we have our Father gave us. We give in gratitude for what we have been given. Jesus said we will be repaid, but we shouldn't put that in too strict a time frame. He also admonished his disciples to "freely give, you have freely received." He also says:

> **When you have done all that is commanded you, say, "We are unworthy servants; we have only done what was our duty."**
> **—Luke 17:10**

Twos need to hear that hard truth because they are prone to see themselves as going beyond the call of duty and expecting to be repaid for it—here and now, emotionally.

At stake in a specific way for the Two is the location of the psychological center of gravity. Unless we look to God as our origin and for our marching orders, we feel empty and insubstantial. Over a period of time this becomes intolerable and they look outside themselves for substance. Twos report having feelings of emptiness in their chests, for example. They can feel lost, confused, and in need of someone else to define them. If that someone is God, who is more inner to us than we are to ourselves, as Augustine said, the Two retains a center inside. But if God is not center, the center will be in the person or group they expect to validate their parking ticket on the planet. It's as though a certain stability and density of being is conferred by our relationship to God.

Prayer affirms and strengthens who we are by clarifying where we stand in relationship to God. Contemplative prayer in which they emotionally bask in the Father's love is good for Twos, and they can often do it very well. The emotional component is developed in them, and emotional prayer can give them the inner density and security they need to detach a bit from other people's approval and feedback.

Twos should watch how children grow. A child grows in love and inner security by knowing she is loved, not by calculating what she needs to do to build self-esteem. "Building self-esteem" is an unfortunate expression. A biblical understanding would lead us to say, more correctly, "discovering self-esteem." A child discovers she is beautiful and valuable and inwardly rich by seeing the appreciative faces of the adults who love her. A Two has to continue this process by dwelling on the face of God, who delights in creation. For that reason, emotional devotional prayer is often helpful for a Two.

Twos in the ministry without a rich prayer-life are a hazard to all concerned. Ministry can institutionalize their investment policy if they have no strong central mooring in prayer. They can value themselves by the position the victims of their ministry give them at the church table. When they do that, they scheme to get the desired positions and they're off and running, instead of standing still and loving.

The Two-based energy is exemplified politically in the stories of the court prophets in the Old Testament, whose relationships with their kings detail this compulsion. They resolve the problem not with parable, but with prayer, which is ultimately what Jesus hopes parables will push his disciples to do.

The pattern in the Old Testament was typical of Middle Eastern royalty of their day. The king had his court of advisors and these advisors included some prophets. In such a court, the

all-important thing is to keep the king's favor. To fall out of favor
is to die. Kings had the unsavory custom of slaughtering "wrong"
prophets, whose sacrifice was then said to have appeased the
very gods the wrong prophets had represented.

Twos often find themselves in the position of these prophets
because they are often attracted to powerful people through
whom they live. In our culture this is especially encouraged for
women: Powerful men attract women who are allowed no life of
their own, no place at the table of the kingdom. These women live
for and through their husbands or employers. And subtler versions of such living through others exist for men and women
alike. Wherever a strict hierarchy (ecclesiastical, political, or fiscal)
prevails, where someone in power can assign places at the table
of life, this dynamic lurks. Twos flourish there.

In the Scriptures the king surrounded himself with advisors who depended on him totally. The result was predictable.
He attracted the Two energies of his advisors. They became
skilled at meeting his needs, as we all become skilled at what
enables us to survive. The first coin of the realm became flattery.
The secret to success was to tell the king how great he was and
how successful he was, or, more important, would be. So when
the king was deliberating on starting a war, he would go to his
prophets. They would prophesy success, if they thought he wanted to fight and failure if they thought he really didn't.

A clear example, by contrast, was the prophet Amos, who
predicted all sorts of terrible things:

> **As the shepherd rescues from the mouth of the lion two**
> **legs, or a piece of an ear, so shall the people of Israel**
> **who dwell in Samaria be rescued with the corner of a**
> **couch and parts of a bed.**
>
> **—Amos 3:12**

In other words, if the king went to war, all that would be left of
Israel would be fragments.

But Amos said of himself:

> **I am no prophet, nor a prophet's son; but I am a herds-**
> **man, and a dresser of sycamore trees, and the Lord took**

me from following the flock, and said to me, "Go, prophesy to my people, Israel."

—**Amos 7:14**

Amos thus pits his relationship with the Lord against the prophets who were for hire. He argues that he is prophesying correctly because he is not a court flatterer in the hire of the king. He is responding to the word of God, doing what Jesus would later call "doing what he sees the Father doing."

The suggestion is the same one Jesus used: The only way not to depend on the assignment of esteem and status by others is to attune oneself to the will of God.

The Two, prone to flattery but with hidden disdain for the person he or she is flattering, can reach emotional honesty by securing his or her position in life only in reference to God.

That is difficult for some, but Jesus' technique is to tell a parable that ruins the effort. Then a Two is free to turn to God.

WHAT CAN A TWO DO?

1) Do several small but symbolic things for people that nobody will find out you are responsible for (not letting your left hand know what your right hand does). Notice all the ways you think of to tell that person what you've secretly done. You will be highly creative and probably fantasize about the person finding out and thanking you profusely. Can you let go of even that?

2) Spend as much time as you can in solitary prayer for several weeks. (Twos feel a lot of pressure from others, so to find out your inner truth, you'll need solitude away from that pressure.) Then read a Gospel in its entirety and notice how much Jesus had to be alone to pray.

3) Make two lists of people: those who drain your energy and those who give you energy. Now make some decisions about time and friendship. Then read the Gospel and notice how Jesus corrected the wrong notions about his identity.

Threes

HIGH-PERFORMANCE ENGINES

Threes are the beautiful people of our country. They are high-energy, high-achieving, efficient, hard-working performers. The power centers of America find Threes over-represented. They rise to the top.

Healthy Threes have the virtues that lead them to success. They set goals with the focus of a stalking cat. They love challenges and solve problems aggressively. They know how to get things done and are willing to do what is necessary to get them done.

They are attractive people, frequently having a keen eye for style and knowledge of the latest fashions. They can create an image with clothes, they can make dining out a culinary event and turn the mundane into the memorable. All with grace and charm.

Healthy Threes are charismatic. When they come into the room the lights seem brighter, the music faster, and the wine more expensive. Happy is the organization run by healthy Threes. Things will get done on time, the marketing will be slick, and the pay will be good.

The sin of the Three is subtle. It is falling in love with the show they're so good at displaying. It is called vanity, or alternatively, deceit, in the Enneagram tradition. When vanity and deceit are synonyms, what is the underlying common denominator? The sin, or distorted worldview, of the Three is the notion that she is worth what she achieves: "I am my trophies." Trophies come in all guises—cars, boats, paintings, certificates, or names to drop. Philosophically, one could say it is a confusion between doing and being. Emotionally, it is the childish belief that if I am a good girl and bring home all "A's" on my report card, my folks will love me. Or at least love me more.

Threes often report that as children, they felt valued for their achievements. These may have been scholastic, artistic, or athletic, but in any case, the recognition would have been for achieving something within the value system of the parents.

Where is deceit in this? Threes don't tell more lies than any other number; instead they sculpt themselves into what they are not. Threes don't go against inner convictions; they hush them. Their agenda is to succeed for whoever is in charge of evaluating success. The deceit comes in a chameleonlike ability to become whatever the situation requires. The agenda is success, but success is contextual. If image is identity, then identity is contextual, too. Threes have places to go and people to be.

If that's a sin, what is wrong with it?

Keeping in mind that a sin isn't something we do, but a power under whose oppression we labor, what's wrong is that it doesn't get Threes what they really want. It is the Three who climbs the corporate ladder to the very top and discovers it is leaning against the wrong wall. A British journalist, teaching in an American school, observed that many of the American students "would eagerly render unto Caesar . . . any Caesar."

WHAT DOES THE THREE WANT?

Three wants to be loved just as she is. A Three believes somewhere down deep that if she embodies the image of the ideal person, then she will be loved. She begins with a false assumption, namely, that she is *not* loved as she is. She sees love as something that must be earned. Her deference to others' wishes takes the center of gravity out of herself. She substitutes their judgment for her own, because "they" measure success. This translates the Three's efforts not only into achievement, but achievement in the eyes of others—an enormous emotional difference.

Three begins to see himself lovable only when he fulfills the expectations of others. The next step, then, is that he, using their criteria, falls in love with his own image. He values, he falls in love with, what he has created: the position, the prestige, the glamor—whatever achievement constituted the image.

Now she is in love with her own image. So it becomes desperately important to maintain that image or she will have nothing to love and no means of gaining love. The stakes are high.

When a Three becomes unhealthy he must maintain the image, whether the reality of achievement is there or not. He becomes vulnerable to shortcuts, sleaze, deception—whatever it takes to keep the image up. Mistakes can't be admitted, failure must be either denied or reframed as "a learning curve," or blamed on someone else. When CEO's talk about their triumphs, they attribute them to hard work, imagination, perseverance, and a bouquet of other virtues. When queried about a recent bankruptcy, the problems are always outside factors: the economy, unfair competition, weather, or communists. Threes don't admit mistakes well. Mistakes are fatal because without success, Threes have nothing.

WHAT THEY SETTLE FOR

Threes settle for image instead of reality. They confuse the two, so it's an easy mistake to make. Their image oppresses the Three. They must serve the image, as though it were the only currency they could exchange for love. When Threes experience love, they are able to free themselves of image. They get real.

America has an historical Calvinist streak that illustrates the worship of achievement in relationship to God. Calvin taught the doctrine of predestination (certain people were chosen before birth to be saved and others to be damned) and many—perhaps most—early American Christians, basing themselves on certain sayings in St. Paul, held the same view.

Here's the rub. When you believe, as a culture, in predestination, a certain itch develops that must be scratched, namely, "Is there any way one can tell if one is among the predestined, the chosen ones?" Slowly it became the conviction of the country that earthly prosperity was one good sign of God's blessing. We still call prosperity a blessing from God (sometimes regardless of how we get it). As a Three culture, we assume poor people are morally inferior. If you don't think so, offer two letters of recommendations to get into college or a job: one from your banker and another from a homeless person you fed. See which one carries the most weight. Or run for public office based on visible support from one of these two groups. Or drop their names and occupations to the parents of the woman you are courting (or those of the man courting you). The context is flexible, the principle is stable: Wealth symbolizes that God loves you (or that you are a good person, which amounts to about the same thing).

Characteristically, Three's addiction needs are infinite. You never get enough of what you really don't want. If you are rich, you need to invest your money and get richer. We have whole industries based on that principle. John Paul Getty, whose name is synonymous with fabulous wealth, had pay phones in his halls for his friends and confided to an interviewer that he felt poor all his life because he was up against richer corporations and he was just one person. He felt poor, but the corporations weren't the reason. On the other hand, when you experience real love, it is enough just to stay in the experience.

Three's addiction to success is not limited to money. In Jesus' society, success was more likely prestige rather than wealth. A classic example occured when the mother of the sons of Zebedee came up to Jesus and begged him:

> "Command that these two sons of mine may sit, one at your right hand and one at your left, in your kingdom." But Jesus answered, "You do not know what you are asking. Are you able to drink the cup that I am to drink?" They said to him, "We are able." He said to them, "You will drink my cup, but to sit at my right hand and at my left is not mine to grant, but it is for those for whom it has been prepared by my Father." And when the ten heard it, they were indignant at the two brothers. But Jesus called them to him and said, "You know that the rulers of the Gentiles lord it over them, and their great men exercise authority over them. It shall not be so among you; but whoever would be great among you must

be your servant, and whoever would be first among you must be your slave; even as the Son of man came not to be served, but to serve, and to give his life as a ransom for many."
—Matthew 20:20-28

So, like the sons of Zebedee, Threes settle for being Number One. Number One in America means workaholism, expensive clothes and cars, physical beauty—any symbol of success will do. Enneagram energy is always symbolic; here it becomes socially obvious. The parable for achieving greatness is again about breaking this type's mind-set. But trying to be first (Number One) by being last, or being a slave, doesn't work, of course. Try it. Try to achieve earthly fame and fortune by serving others. How will it work? Reducing the parable to technique by taking it literally will ruin it. You might as well try to achieve resurrection by killing yourself.

But if you let the dynamic settle into you—to value service as much as conquest—you will rearrange values, energies, and perspectives. Human society is always structured, and in Jesus' perspective, it is always structured wrong. So his inversion is always going on, always forcing us into new growth. This certainly makes success difficult: Today's success prevents tomorrow's movement. We even say "You can't argue with success." But Threes need to know that Jesus argues with it all the time.

If you're lucky, you may never have heard of the DSM-IV. The IV just refers to Volume 4, the DSM means Diagnostic and Statistical Manual. This is a large book that classifies mental illnesses according to clusters of malfunction. Therapists can't bill insurance companies without paperwork that includes the DSM-IV classification.

All of the Enneagram types have, with more or less congruence, a DSM-IV equivalent. Twos are called hysterical, type Sevens are manic-depressive, and so on. But Threes are unique on the Enneagram diagram in that the Three pathology has no DSM equivalent.

Why not? Because The United States is a type Three country. Countries, families, corporations, and parishes—any group that hangs together for a long time—develop a fairly recognizable Enneagram type. The United States manifests a Three trance that makes it difficult to see the trance of the individual Three. Threeness is protective coloration in the United States.

Jesus tells a parable that challenges the American way of life and type Threes:

> For the Kingdom of heaven is like a householder who went out early in the morning to hire laborers for his vineyard. After agreeing with the laborers for a denarius a day, he sent them into his vineyard. And going out about the third hour he saw others standing idle in the market place; and to them he said, "You go into the vineyard too, and whatever is right I will give you." So they went. Going out again about the sixth hour and the ninth hour, he did the same. And about the eleventh hour he went and found others standing; and he said to them, "Why do you stand here idle all day?" They said to him, "Because no one has hired us." He said to them, "You go into the vineyard too." And when evening came, the owner of the vineyard said to his steward, "Call the laborers and pay them their wages, beginning with the last, up to the first." And when those hired about the eleventh hour came, each of them received a denarius. Now when the first came, they thought they would receive more; but each of them also received a denarius. And on receiving it they grumbled at the householder, saying, "These last worked only one hour, and you have made them equal to us who have borne the burden of the day and the scorching heat." But he replied to one of them, "Friend, I am doing you no wrong; did you not agree with me for a denarius? Take what belongs to you, and go; I choose to give to this last as I give to you. Am I not allowed to do what I choose with what belongs to me? Or do you begrudge my generosity? So the last will be first, and the first last."

—Matthew 20:1–16

The legal end of the argument holds up. Our Father can be generous if he wants. But organized labor would not accept this as fair employment practice. Of all the parables in the scriptures, this is one I have heard people dare criticize the most. Most people take the parables as mystical sayings or moral suggestions, but this one talks about money and wages and we all know about that in the United States, so we feel we have a right to speak up. More subtly, we dare to speak up because we *know* what is right here, because we are speaking out of a cultural consensus. We argue among ourselves about some things, but when there is cultural agreement, we are sure we are right.

The parable offers access to the kingdom to everyone, regardless of their performance or their time in the field.

This is why the parable is so important for Threes. Threes have a personal belief that has been condemned as a heresy for centuries. The heresy is that same Pelagianism mentioned in the previous chapter. It was named for the monk, Pelagius, who promulgated the belief that we could perfect ourselves without the help of grace. Pelagius believed instead in a rather strict relationship between our moral activity and our being pleasing to God.

But the parable unties the strings of a carefully wrapped package of unhealthy beliefs that America and most other Threes have. The first and most destructive belief is that until we do something for God, we are not delightful to her. God's love is something we have to earn.

If children hold such a view, they believe that until they earn their parents' love, they are of no value. Threes equate being with achieving. They also believe that they will be loved just to the extent they perform a valuable service for someone else.

Threes get a lot of social energy from this belief. After all if your (love) life depends on achieving, you get good at it. But there is a spiritual price to be paid. Because Threes are so dependent on achieving, they give their souls over to those who are in a position to recognize, reward, and define achievement.

Threes silence their souls to hear the demands of a high-performance life. The interior life, where no one give rewards or evaluations, but where personal stability actually lies, atrophies.

Another problem Threes have, both personally and in America, is forgiveness. For commerce to work, justice must prevail. And justice does not consider the heart. It considers behavior and the same objective standards must apply to all. In such a context, of course, forgiveness plays no part. Police do not forgive burglars, nor do the victims. Merchants seldom forgive debts. You can hear the cultural voice all around us: "If we give money to those welfare mothers, they'll just keep having babies to get the money." Notice the cultural (and very un-Christian) presupposition: "They are bad until they do good things to prove they are good." And the smug supporting piece reads, "I have performed, so I am good and they should be like I am." The wealthier and more successful—and more entranced as a Three type—one is, the clearer this conviction.

Competition plagues many Threes. America's cruelty to people who fail is rooted in a Three-based worldview that success is the ultimate source of meaning. If you can be Number One in anything, you have worth. Look at the bizarre popularity of the *Guinness Book of Records* and how much exertion is spent trying to get in it. The *Book of Records* validates those people who need to compete at whatever they do.

Competition is ultimately heartbreaking. Being Number One only lasts until the next season; only one team out of dozens gets to be Number One. The rest are consigned to oblivion. In America a silver medal can be highly ambiguous. "You know, with a little luck (or a little more practice or better coach or whatever), I could have gotten the gold." A few athletes can rejoice in the silver, but they probably aren't Threes.

Competition writes the Three trance in large letters. The prize is awarded by others; the rules are the same for all regardless of advantages, only success is rewarded, not effort or integrity or perseverance. Compassion for the loser is absent. "Winner take all" is a cultural barbarism practiced and taught in our school system and perfected in professional sports. We spend fortunes on a few gifted athletes and ignore bodily health to a large extent. If you can't compete, get out of the game.

What is really destructive is the number of coaches, teachers, media spokespersons and others who see games as "more than a game, a way of life." Sad to say, they are absolutely right. And the game is the Three's trance. In games, the first shall be first, but in the kingdom, the last shall be first and the first last. This paradox doesn't make sense in a literal way, of course, because if you took it literally, then all you would need to do to succeed is to fail. That looks easy on a literal level, but as you failed, you would secretly be trying to succeed and now you're caught by the first half of the paradox. A lovely Three solvent.

On a deeper level, Jesus is saying there is no first or last. God loves all of us unconditionally and doesn't love one any more than another. Competition presumes comparison, but God's point of making individuals is that there is no comparison. We can compress certain levels of tasks and skills, but envision a competitive prayer meet or competitive compassion and you see how the deeper things in life don't allow comparison. Jesus insists we go to these deeper levels and be concerned with these deeper truths.

It isn't accidental that America treats its poor so shabbily, executes more of its poor (we execute poor criminals, but not rich ones) than any other nation, and its correctional institutions boast they are the "fastest-growing industry in America." When personal worth depends on achievement, forgiveness is unthinkable.

That's why the parable is such a threat to the Three's mindset. No objective standards were observed, people stood around all day and didn't get fined, and superior (at least longer) performance was not rewarded.

In many senses, both America and Threes in general try too hard. Threes work too hard. If something doesn't work, Americans just try harder. Notice how that slogan "We Try Harder," caught everyone's attention. We are so worried about Japan's superior corporate skills that politicians and educators are planning to have our children go to school the year around. We offer our workers one or two weeks vacation, maybe three after they are gray. But in Europe, five and six weeks are the norm. A number of sources report that a major health problem in America is shortage of sleep. Threes are workaholic, as is America. The parable assaults the system that rewards workaholics and so is offensive to many.

The earliest form of earning God's love in the Hebrew Scriptures was sacrifice. Catholics who are raised on the presentation of the Eucharist as sacrifice don't give much thought to the earlier forms of sacrifice. It began with human sacrifice, and then moved to temple sacrifice. An entire culture was built around the temple. It was the pivot of Jewish life. When Jesus attacked the whole temple system on a number of occasions, we don't make much of it, but the underlying dynamic is crucial.

The notion that we earn God's love by sacrifice pervades the Hebrew Scriptures and was dominant in the pagan religions of the time. It still lingers in our liturgy at times and is common in popular piety. We "give things up" for Lent. That kind of talk is returning and it feels good to many. It gives some control over how well God is going to like us. Certainly our efforts must be important! Threes hold this idea and make it social. Certainly, if we do all the right things, both God and humanity will love us. And the harder we work, the better. The more love we will earn. Love is a strenuous task for Threes. William James, the brilliant American psychologist, couldn't shake his American Three-based belief and defined religion as "the strenuous life."

Jesus took the Pharisees to task for making life strenuous for the people, and for Three-like reasons. He tells his disciples:

> **They bind heavy burdens, hard to bear, and lay them on men's shoulders; but they themselves will not move them with their finger. They do all their deeds to be seen by men. . . .**
>
> **—Matthew 23:4**

"To be seen by men" is the Three's temptation. Contrast that with Jesus' words to the disciples:

> **Come to me, all who labor and are heavy-ladened, and I will give you rest. Take my yoke upon you, and learn from me, for I am gentle and lowly in heart; and you will find rest for your souls. For my yoke is easy, and my burden light.**
>
> **—Matthew 11:28–30**

This paradox frustrates the Three's Enneagram agenda. How can a yoke be easy? Yokes are, by definition, what one shoulders to plow a field or carry water. And since when is a burden light? To the extent it is light, it is not a burden. What shall Threes do now when life is easy? If achievement is love, an easy life is a loveless one. The interchangeability of love and work gets cruelly acted out in the lives of Three workaholics.

When anything is done from a context of realized love, of psychological fullness, it is easy. If love seems too sublime an answer, watch a group of boys wanting to play ball. What they most want is to exert themselves because they love the game. A musician will play, not work, a difficult piece of music. Anything done out of love, regardless of effort, becomes easy. Without love, all is work. But for the Three, with love at stake in the performance, work is an investment, not an exercise of plenitude.

The more labors are visible and rewarding, the more apt Threes are to confuse success with approval of God. But Jesus came to sinners, not the just, which in this context means that God's love is extended to anyone who will accept it. Those most likely to accept it are those who admit a certain need. Those who are honest. One of the fine things about the Enneagram is that it convicts each of us of our sin. That puts us in a good position to be open to grace.

Sacrifice is central to some religious experience, but it is a powerful and dangerous tradition. It seizes central importance in any scheme that appeases, controls, or even suggests some kind of leverage over divine favor. Threes offer their time and effort as their sacrifice to gain both human and divine love. Sacrifice is dangerous because it corrodes any relationship, human or divine. Parents sacrifice for their children, but it is out of a sense of care and love, not to gain their affection. If they do it to gain affection, as an investment, it destroys the relationship. If they remind the children of their sacrifice, they are often surprised when the children respond with ingratitude and even hostility.

If the children sacrifice to gain approval from their parents, it is even more clearly destructive. Yet that was primitive religion and the pattern that Jesus came to break: "I desire mercy and not sacrifice."

The drivenness of the Three needs to be balanced with rest and contemplation. Especially for the Three, contemplation is resting in the knowledge that God loves unconditionally.

Psalm 51 links forgiveness and an anti-sacrificial attitude beautifully. The Psalmist begins by asking forgiveness and acknowledging sin:

> **Have mercy on me, O God, according to thy steadfast love.**

Notice the mercy comes because of God's love, not human endeavor. The Psalmist continues :

> **For I know my transgressions, and my sin is ever before me. Against thee, thee only, have I sinned and done that which is evil in thy sight.**

He continues with beautiful repentant poetry and then adds, perhaps surprisingly to us, in verses 16 and 17:

> **For thou hast no delight in sacrifice; were I to give a burnt offering, thou wouldst not be pleased. The sacrifice acceptable to God, is a broken spirit; a broken and contrite heart, O God, thou wilt not despise.**

(The last two verses talk about the restoration of proper sacrifices, but they are later additions to make the psalm more palatable to the priests for whom sacrifice was a means of livelihood.)

The pattern of forgiveness followed by good behavior runs throughout the ministry of Jesus. He never asks for anything before forgiveness, always (if he asks anything at all) after. The Three assumes the contrary, that one must do good things first if one is to be forgiven. Jesus' phrase in Matthew 9:13 that "I have come to call sinners, not the just," usually goes right past Threes as mysterious hyperbole.

Threes can experience a loss of self as they meet the expectations of others. It is as though their center of gravity lay outside themselves. "I am who they think I am." The mechanism by which they become a pseudo-self is mimicry. Threes adopt the styles, manners, convictions, and attitudes of the important people in society.

Because Threes are addicted to success and the system that defines it, they have an inner formula for obtaining it. It begins with the conviction that they are not loved, living in a world of scarcity in which there isn't enough love. (Economic law of supply and demand has the same belief system; Threes understand economics and frequently do well making money). Threes, after giving up on being loved for themselves, work very hard to earn the love of parents, teachers, bosses, and God. They work hard to earn something that resembles love but really isn't. When Threes are told they are loved, they discount it, saying to themselves, "They bought the act. They bought the image."

The gospel frequently emphasizes being over doing, contemplation over action, and observing the Sabbath over productivity. Threes don't really understand the Sabbath (or Sunday) as a day of rest. They are restless, all over the United States, to open the stores on Sunday, keep factories open twenty-four hours a day, and keep the economy hot. The biblical tradition struggles to get us to take a day off, to be still and know God, to stop work long enough to pray. Jesus said to pray always. That is not possible literally, but a command that clarifies the priority to be given to the interior life. Threes have a difficult time with that cryptic statement; they would do well to take it to heart.

WHAT CAN A THREE DO?

1) Pamper yourself with some time off because you're already good enough. Try Sunday. Add some sensual pleasure just because you deserve it.

2) Of the people you love the most, how many of them earned your love by doing something for you?

3) Read Luke's gospel from beginning to end. Then ask yourself why Jesus seems to have special affection for the poor. Whether you understand that economically or spiritually, that affection still conflicts with your Enneagram agenda.

4) Go and watch new parents with their baby. What does the baby have to do to earn their love? How old are you in the

eyes of God? (Remember, God is more than fifteen billion years old!)

5) Walk through a mall. Notice how many people are old, ugly, deformed, out of fashion, or otherwise unattractive—to you. Did God make a lot of mistakes? Or is there another order of affection going on here?

Fours

THE UNIVERSE LOVED YOU BETTER

If "everybody" thinks that Threes are the beautiful people, the really discerning few think the Fours are beautiful.

Fours are richly emotional with an appreciation for beauty and drama that gives them a flair we usually associate with artists. They are sensitive, often making excellent counselors when healthy. They won't run from your (or their own) emotional pain. They hang in, understanding a special value in suffering.

Fours have considerable emotional range; they are equally at home in ecstasy and emotional shipwreck. They often have richly aesthetic lives, regardless of their talent. They need and usually find meaning in aesthetic pursuits. They value being original and unique and spend time and emotional energy in the pursuit of authenticity. It is more important to a Four that she be authentic, true to herself, than that she please others, whatever their authority.

Fours take their inner life seriously. They can spend hours analyzing and processing their inner moods and feelings. With this inner focus their immediate environment can be an obsession with them because they modulate their inner mood swings with it.

When Enneagram therapist Tom Condon noted that Fours feel like they're from another planet, I thought it a fine striking hyperbole. Then a month ago a Four friend of mine looked across the lunch table at me and said emotionally, "I feel like I'm from another planet!"

Fours can be among the most emotionally alienated of the Enneagram spaces. They feel defective and often report a physical or emotional abandonment at any early age. The consequence of this experience is a sense of not fitting in anywhere, of being wrong at the core, of being unworthy of love. At the same time they feel unworthy of love, they also believe that if they ever could find the perfect love, they would be blissfully happy forever.

But when love comes to the Four, he discounts it because of course, he is not worthy. What is true of his human relationships is equally true of his relationship to God. Fours often have serious guilt problems and low self-esteem. They take the words of the Centurion in the Gospel of Luke literally:

> . . . **Lord, do not trouble yourself, for I am not worthy that you should come under my roof.**
>
> —Luke 7:6

They have more difficulty with the last half of the sentence:

> **Say but the word and let my servant be healed.**

They don't really want to be healed because their unworthiness and emotional distress is a means of making a claim on others.

WHAT THEY WANT

What Fours want more than anything else in life is love in the form of a perfect relationship. They want to be loved perfectly. They are intensely emotional and they nurture the belief that if they can have the perfect relationship, they will be definitively happy. Along with this belief that love will make them happy goes an irrational belief that one day they did have such a relationship and there was a time when they were blissfully in love.

WHAT THEY SETTLE FOR

The sin of the Four is envy. What does envy get them? Why should they want what others have? For the Four, envy is a means of gaining this perfect love. Envy creates the vacuum that entitles them to be filled.

Their center of gravity lies outside themselves. It is others who have love; they themselves do not. It is the others who must love them to happiness.

It's a bit complicated, but the Four gives away her sense of being worthy, of being loved. She gives it away by saying or thinking that others have what is rightfully hers. Once she has given it away, she scurries about trying to get it back. She does this by declaring that because what is rightfully hers has been stolen, she deserves to be loved because of her need. Envy creates a vacuum that God and other perfect lovers must fill.

So the Four settles for *deserving* the perfect relationship. He makes almost a moral demand on the universe that the perfect relationship be supplied. The Four heats up his inner life until the emotions are steaming. He cultivates an authenticity that is frequently spiritual and he feels that this makes him worthy of a perfect love.

But the posture is envy, creating a feeling of lacking something to attract the perfect love. The Four can often try to turn this defect into uniqueness in the hopes of further establishing her claim to perfect love. The first thing any lover knows to do is to tell the beloved that he or she is different from all others. Fours feel this difference vividly.

Fours indulge in a type of manipulation. They recount, in vivid and extended detail, just how terrible their life is *as a means of gaining love*. They tell others how bad things are, so that they will feel sorry for them. They also are expected to do something about it—to at least admire how sensitive Fours are because of their suffering. Their sensitivity both causes and is caused by their intense suffering. We call this litany of woes "lamentations." Personal suffering is a badge of honor, making them unique. Pain opens portals to depths unknown to ordinary, insensitive folks. Pain is a claim on the universe and God for an outpouring of love.

For this reason, many Fours love the lamentation psalms. Fully a third of the Psalms are woe-recitals, and Fours particularly appreciate them. The understanding in these psalms was that to complain to God was to invoke divine help. The worse one's situation, the more deserving he or she was.

The lamentations don't chronicle one's moral fault; they are not confessions of sin. They are a description of how terrible life is. Seen against the background of the belief that God vindicates his righteous ones, the lamentations are a protest that bad things are happening to a good person. God, being infinitely just, will surely not allow this situation to exist for long.

One of the most famous of these, Psalm 22, is incorporated in the Good Friday liturgy:

> **My God, my God, why hast thou forsaken me?**
> **Why are you so far from helping me, from my groaning?**
> **My God, I cry by day, but you don't answer;**
> **and by night but find no rest.**
> **Yet you are holy, enthroned on the praises of Israel.**
> **In you our fathers trusted and you delivered them.**
> **They cried to you and weren't disappointed.**
>
> **But I am a worm and no man;**
> **scorned by men and despised by the people.**
> **All who see me mock me**
> **They scoff at me and wag their heads.**
>
> **—Psalm 22:1–8**

The psalmist continues for thirty verses, sixty lines, vividly describing how he is suffering and how he trusts that the Lord will deliver him.

The Hebrew Scriptures did not believe in resurrection, nor in heaven and hell as Christians understand those terms, so divine justice had to happen here and now. The Book of Job pushes this belief to the limits and finally gives up, declaring that we just don't know the ways and will of God. But until we do know, the Four will lament until given love.

The Jewish culture displays some strong Four-like characteristics. Lamentation, the Four's favorite literary style, was raised to an art form in the Psalms, and in Jerusalem the Jews built a monument to misery, the Wailing Wall. The custom prevails today to stand by the Wailing Wall and howl to heaven, expressing the profound agony suffered because of the lack of justice in the world about which God should do something.

Like all Enneagram strategies, type Four sees a world in which love is at a premium. An acute shortage of love prompts the Four to blame himself for the shortage. When he blames himself, he devalues himself and accounts himself as having no direct way to obtain love. At the same time, Fours tend to look back on a golden age when love was abundant. (In the Scriptures this is the Garden of Eden before the Fall.) The Four simultaneously blames himself and tells himself that others have this love that he misses so forlornly. The strategy is to reframe the melancholy into a badge of entitlement. "Because I have it so bad, I am entitled to whatever little consolation I can get." "Life is not fair, others have what I can't get."

For many Fours the sense of abandonment and corresponding helplessness translates into an inability to want to work in the external world. Just to revel in ever-deepening pools of emotional richness can be enough. Talented Four artists and writers talk of a block of their artistic powers.

One can imagine the shock to such a worldview the following parable would be:

> I tell you, do not be anxious about your life, what you shall eat, nor about your body, what you shall put on. For life is more than food, and the body more than clothing. Consider the ravens: they neither sow nor reap, they have neither storehouse nor barn, and yet God feeds them. Of how much more value are you than the birds! And which of you by being anxious can add a cubit to his span of life? If then you are not able to do as small a thing as that, why are you anxious about the rest? Consider the lilies, how they grow; they neither toil nor spin; yet I tell you, even Solomon in all his glory was not arrayed like one of these. But if God so clothes the grass which is alive in the field today and tomorrow is thrown into the oven, how much more will he clothe you, O you of little faith.
>
> —Matthew 6:25–30

This parable undoes the Four's worldview in a number of ways. First it begins, as do many of Jesus' Kingdom parables, with a sense that the world is all right the way it is. It tells the Four, "You have what you need." Keep in mind, this is not economic policy or advice on how to live. It is an insight into our relationship to God. When Jesus talks in parables, he uses metaphors of daily life to explain our relationship to God.

In the first line, Jesus gives away the level on which he is speaking. He says, "Don't be anxious about your life." What can that mean? It almost has to mean that he is speaking about something more important than life itself. In Jesus' view, our relationship to God is more important than life. He believed that and accordingly, out of integrity, died. The early Church placed enormous value on martyrdom because it believed Jesus: the coming of the kingdom was more important than life.

The mystic Julian of Norwich's most famous saying is "All will be well, all will be well, all manner of things will be well." Until you are a mystic like Jesus and Julian, that may seem like nonsense. Children die of starvation, AIDS spreads unchecked, we've killed 200,000,000 people in wars this century. Therefore what on earth can it mean to say, "All manner of things will be well"? It means that in some ultimate sense, the story will come out right. Mystics see that ultimate sense.

All manner of philosophers and theologians grant that we have no rational answer to the mystery of evil. What Jesus and Julian apparently are able to do is see beyond the evil to another greater good. Whether we decide to simply trust the mystery of life or have a more concrete vision of heaven, where all the tears will be wiped away, is a matter of what form our faith takes.

But it is clear that Jesus has a vision of fullness embodied in his parables that directly undoes the private scenario of each of the Enneagram styles. In this Four style, the deprived view of the world devalues the self. The understanding seems to be that "If I were valuable, I wouldn't have been abandoned. But I was, so I'm worthless."

But Jesus says:

Of how much more value are you than the birds.

—Matthew 6:26

The kingdom vision of Jesus says that we will be taken care of because we are valuable.

If the parable is taken as fiscal strategy, of course it is absurd. But the absurdity hasn't stopped multitudes from doing just that. The meaning of the parable that reveals the fullness of Jesus' vision is that there is plenty of love: Even the plants get it. Fours need to believe this, but usually don't. Instead of asking for what they want directly, because they are valuable and because they are loved, they chart out a circuitous route to arrive at being valuable. They confess they are without value, and then claim entitlement because they are the only ones without value. Everybody else is valued; they alone are downtrodden.

Sin is not enjoyable. Sin oppresses us and it is beyond our power to deal with it by ourselves. The sin of envy is no exception. The sin of envy simultaneously puts ourselves down and elevates the other. This is not fair. When the situation is not fair, direct measures don't work. So the Four develops a distorted sense of entitlement.

The sin of envy is obliterated if one can accept the parable. The parable is the forgiveness of the sin. The parable says there is no deprived world. There is plenty of love to go around. Look how God loves ravens and lilies and grass. This is a sign that we all are loved; not one of us is abandoned. We don't need to struggle to restore what we think we lost.

Of course, neither a Four nor anyone else is going to go through this careful analysis of what is involved.

But what does happen when Fours read this parable is that it conflicts dramatically with the way they feel about the world. They experience anxiety, even despair, about earning enough money, about doing anything in the world, about being valuable, about the state of the universe. Fours need to reconcile the profound melancholy they feel with the words of Jesus not to be anxious even about life itself. Mothers tell children all the time, "Everything is going to be all right." We need a "second naiveté" to return as adults to what is true in that statement.

It is the obvious unreasonableness of the parable if taken literally that makes it effective. When Jesus presents a parable to us and it doesn't make sense on a literal level, we are forced to a

higher synthesis. Fours, in this case, have made a premature clo-
sure of life. Like all fixations and games, the choice they've made
is a closed self-validating loop. Fours didn't get into the loop
rationally and won't get out of it that way either. Trying to "talk
them out of it" is doomed and all efforts to cheer them up will
seem patronizing and infuriating to them. Sevens are especially
troublesome to Fours when they try to cheer them up this way.
The Seven's optimism seems shallow to the melancholy Four.

Jesus doesn't put any stock in rational persuasion. He simply offers another view of life. This puts the believing Four in a
delicious bind. Either hang on to your deprived view of the
world and justify your convoluted efforts to compensate, or trust
Jesus beyond what you can see and in doing so become free. The
parable requests faith. It does so by presenting a vision of what
life would be like if you believed that God loves you. That's the
ultimate meaning of :

You will know the truth and the truth will make you free.

—John 8:32

Like any game, the Four's game has emotional payoffs that pre-
clude the real rewards of life. The emotional payoff is a feeling of
authenticity. The rest of us, who do not know how terrible life is,
are living in a fool's paradise. Jean-Paul Sartre, the famous French
existentialist philosopher, said that to become conscious was to
become nauseous. Fours believe that.

So for the Four, to be melancholy and nauseated is to be
authentic. This is the inner conviction of the Four. They want to
be authentic with great emotional intensity. They don't recognize
the feeling of authenticity as a secondary gain in a game that
costs them love. Pop religion preaches that the only thing they
need for real faith is sincerity. The delusional component of sincerity is not faced, probably because sincerity can be arrived at
without reference to any external reality. Any action can feel sincere. That's why it is such a special trap for the Four; it appeals
to their need for authenticity.

For the Fours, the Enneagram functions well as an orthodoxy. By "orthodoxy" here I mean an objective standard by

which behavior, emotions, worldviews, and spiritual health are all judged. Fours need an objective standard so they don't sink into formless emotional vagaries. Fours often love the Enneagram because they find out their tormented world is not the norm and they are not alone in it. Once they learn they have constructed a deprived world, they have hope that they can deconstruct it. The parables are so effective because they deconstruct a deprived and tormented world.

Jesus also said that our tormented world is not the norm and we are not alone in it. He put the center of gravity outside ourselves. In the Beatitudes, Jesus repeats:

You have heard that it was said to the men of old . . . but I say to you . . .
—Matthew 5:21

But Fours should read the Beatitudes with a certain caution. The blessing of those who mourn, who are poor in spirit, the meek —they pose a certain temptation to the Four. The Fours feel that life has been unfair to them and they will emotionally identify with the underdog who is going to be given what they need. They are all too ready to have their mourning turned into joy by someone else.

Repentance means giving up one's deprived and tormented worldview. It means challenging a previous belief system, long before it means stopping a certain behavior. You will notice that for the fullness of the kingdom to break into one's life (in the form of healing miracles), Jesus always required faith, not proof of moral rectitude. That's because the morality will flow from the vision of fullness. People aren't immoral for the fun of it; they do it to survive in a world of perceived scarcity.

When Fours have moral problems, they usually flow from this distorted sense of entitlement. Their sin, envy, is called in scholastic tradition, a capital sin. *Capital* means "head" sin in the sense that it is the sin from which the others flow. From Four's distorted sense of entitlement comes their other moral problems. It is easy to see how a Four could justify sensual consolation for their lamentation-articulated misery. And more commonly, they could justify aesthetic extravagance to prop up their feeling of inner deprivation. Once the playing field is made uneven by envy, compensation follows easily. It feels like getting even with life's unfairness. And if your prayer has been a careful litany of that unfairness, you're set up. Unhealthy Fours have a pronounced sense of entitlement that often gets them into trouble.

Another parable that undoes the Four's worldview states :

> Will any one of you who has a servant plowing or keeping sheep say to him when he has come in from the field, "Come at once and sit down at table!" Will he not rather say to him, "Prepare supper for me, and gird yourself and serve me, till I eat and drink; and afterward you shall eat and drink"? Does he thank the servant because he did what was commanded? So you also, when you have done all that is commanded you, say, "We are unworthy servants; we have only done what was our duty."
>
> —Luke 17:7–10.

Like so many, this is a parable of the kingdom, of grace. No matter how morally good one is (in the Four's case, how emotionally authentic and sincere), there is no claim on God. There is no great honor in just doing what we're told. Good behavior only raises us to the level of an unprofitable servant. This is in sharp contrast with the real gift of grace which makes one a child of God, not a servant.

This is another attack on the Four-based way of earning love. Fours can't lay emotional claims to love just by being needy any more than Threes can by being successful. The parable destroys any spiritual power trip. No matter what one does, one is just doing it with what they have been given.

Fours have a tendency to consider themselves special. The parable that categorizes all of us as mere servants is a mild antidote to the subtle preening that goes on when one is really special.

The Jewish nation seems rather Four-like at times, particularly when they are emphasizing their being the chosen people without any reference to why they are chosen. For many Jews, being chosen was understood as being required to do a specific task, namely to make the Lord, Yahweh, known and glorified.

But for a Four-based segment, it meant that the Jews were special, even better. They had something no one else had, and some thought this made them superior. Many Christians carry a similar arrogance today.

It was to these that John the Baptist, when he came preaching repentance, told the crowds:

> . . . and do not begin to say to yourselves, "We have Abraham for our father."
>
> —Luke 3:8

The crowd couldn't claim any specialness because Abraham was their ancestor. That did not excuse them from repentance. They were just like everybody else (just what a Four hates to hear). John's term for "just like everybody else" is poetic:

> God is able out of these stones to raise up children to Abraham.
>
> —Luke 3:8

This lays bare those who clutch the cloak of Abrahamic descent around them. They are on a level with stones! Not much specialness there. Those who resisted repentance on the grounds of genetic superiority resemble the unhealthy Fours who are unable to function well in the world because they are made for more sublime tasks. "After all, one doesn't pull a plow with a Porsche," an unhealthy Four will sniff.

So the Jewish history came full circle: God chose them precisely because they were slaves, had no land, were without military power. He chose them because of what they did not have. And by the time of Jesus, many Jews considered themselves morally superior to the pagans. The same dynamic operates in Fours. They consider themselves special because of their defect and think this vacuum, being abhorred by God and nature alike, will draw the favor of the perfect lover, human or divine, and make them special. Because they are special they will be loved, at last.

That's the Four's game that the call to repentance by John severs at the roots. The Four is not special. She is loved unconditionally by God, just as everybody else is. She doesn't need specialness as a claim. She doesn't need any claim. All she has to do is change her worldview. The parables help.

Jesus himself points out how parables can help. Right after a long explanation of the parable of seed and the sower (the only place where a parable is explained), Jesus says how important it is to listen to parables:

> **Take heed then how you hear; for to him who has will more be given, and from him who has not, even what he thinks that he has will be taken away.**
>
> **—Luke 8:18**

The weight of Jesus' message is that if we listen to parables and take them to heart, we will learn more and more. But if we remain just casual listeners without trying to penetrate their depth, not only will we stay ignorant, but even the wisdom we think we have will be diluted with such half-attention. We will be worse off than when we first heard the parables.

The dynamic Jesus describes applies especially to Fours. Those who succeed in responding to parables will be given further wisdom. Fours can, as in the case of the lamentations, make demands on God because they are inadequate or helpless. But Jesus does not encourage helplessness. He cures people so they can see for themselves; he heals the lame so they can walk themselves. To those who have faith, he grants healing. But those who plead that things are impossible, he accuses of having no faith. Right after this statement about parables, Luke tells the story of the disciples who were frightened when a storm came up and they were adrift in a boat on a lake. They panicked and Jesus admonished them:

> **Where is your faith?**
>
> **—Luke 8:25**

Then Jesus calmed the storm. This kind of affirmation of available power is helpful for Fours to assimilate. It counters their negative appraisal of their situation. They then can pray with confidence without having to indulge in the self-pity to which many of them are prone.

WHAT CAN A FOUR DO?

1) Record an hour of lamentation Psalms and listen to them until you get in touch with the emotional excess.

2) Gratitude to God and your friends expresses and intensifies your inner core of health and beauty. Make it a point to look for things for which you are grateful.

3) Make something—anything—beautiful and meditate on the beauty within you that created it.

4) Humor is a saving grace of healthy Fours. What can you do to develop and enjoy your sense of humor?

Fives

A VERY PRIVATE EYE

Beginning with Buddha, Fives are numbered among those people most dedicated to the search for wisdom. They are capable of a great deal of emotional detachment from their efforts, they value knowledge and its attendant virtues, and they have a serene objectivity that makes them fine teachers, researchers, and writers.

Healthy Fives have a long view of things, they plan well, taking all the details into consideration. They spend a great deal of attention to their interior life, which can result in their being highly sensitive and articulate. They seem mature beyond their years at times, with their deliberate intellectual approach to life.

An eighteen-year-old Five applied for college. His entrance essay was entitled "The Observer." The first line began "I'm invisible." Typical of an intellectual Five, he understood with limpid clarity his own wishes, actions, and responses.

Fives need privacy like small edible animals do, and they feel a little like them. They live in fear of being devoured. A common scenario for a Five is growing up with a fear of invasion. At other times this translates into their having such a powerful intellectual and imaginative inner life that they simply don't want a lot of outside pressures. In any case, they love to be on the edges of action watching, rather than being directly involved.

Fives are the most intellectual of all the numbers. They are careful systematic thinkers who can make real contributions to the world if they can find a way to do it in the form of sharing information.

Perhaps the computer will bring healthy Fives the recognition they deserve. The computer offers low-impact communication for Fives with the specific intellectual component they tend to appreciate.

As keen observers, Fives are often fine writers and reporters. Their domicile of choice is an observational tower. They also make fine counselors when what is needed is insight, objectivity, and a sounding board. But don't expect emotional confrontation from them.

The traditional sin of the Five is avarice, but here again, the Enneagram enlarges the concept. The scholastic tradition understood avarice as hoarding material goods. Enneagram thought today focuses more on the hoarding of time and affection.

What Do Fives Really Want?

The sin of avarice tells us what the Fives really want. They want to be rich. Being rich is their preferred metaphor for the life of abundance that Jesus promised. The first premise of kingdom spirituality is that we live in a world of abundance. Jesus said he came to bring us life, abundant life. Because of their preoccupation with their intellect, Fives sculpt their longing into a search for the riches of the inner life. They create privacy to think and often prefer fantasy to reality. When mental life is primary, virtual reality will often do. They want abundant life, like the rest of us, but they look for it in their heads.

Many absent-minded professors are Fives, preoccupied with their inner life at the expense of what the rest of the world says is more real. Fives can seem very religious; they love contemplation. They also have a natural asceticism because one of their traits is a willingness to live on very little. When they are unhealthy, however, the reason they like to live on very little is that then they think they won't be dependent on others and so won't have to interact with others.

WHAT DO THEY SETTLE FOR?

Instead of the abundance of life, they settle for what they can get in their heads. Fives will often do without sensate pleasures: food, fine clothes, fancy cars, and all that. But they will make every effort to get as much information, and have as rich a fantasy life as they can.

Any trance is a fixation on a few inner realities to the exclusion of the richer broad spectrum of life. The Five trance is publicly recognized as "living in an ivory tower." Fives can live in their heads and ignore social and political and even many physical realities for long periods of time.

The trance is in reaction to fear. Fives are afraid of being overwhelmed. The reason they fear overwhelming is because, despite how they appear to outsiders, they are hypersensitive. Because they are so sensitive, they are easily influenced. So to defend their sensitive souls, they try to escape from various outside influences.

Their trance focuses on the exchange between the inner and the outer world. They are like a body of water that needs to monitor inflow and outflow carefully. They often rehearse what will be coming in so they can handle the experience when it gets there. During the experience, they detach from full participation and observe themselves, and then after the experience, they replay it and analyze it. In a certain way the experience takes on more reality during the replay than it did during the event.

When healthy, they love the exchange of knowledge; they make good teachers if they don't have to divert their efforts from presenting the material to take care of student discipline and motivation. Their way of dealing with the external environment is by understanding it, so they are often found in research or reporting. Fives frequently love to share knowledge, but that can be an ambiguous experience. When one shares knowledge, the knowledge still belongs to him or her, so it is sharing without much emotional cost. But it can be quite healthy, too, because such sharing involves the output of time and energy and attention, which add up to emotional currency of considerable value, especially if the knowledge enriches the listener.

THE PARABLE

Apparently, the most obvious words of Jesus addressed to those who would hoard is the simple injunction:

> Do not lay up for yourselves treasures on earth, where moth and rust consume and where thieves break in and steal, but lay up for yourselves treasures in heaven, where neither moth nor rust consumes and where thieves do not break in and steal. For where your treasure is, there will your heart be also.

> **—Matthew 6:19–21**

But Fives can easily get around this straight moral command by withdrawing from the economic struggle and living on little or nothing. Their trance is more conservative than acquisitive. They tend not to spend money, but they don't tend to take the kind of high-profile jobs that earn them the rewards that thieves would relish. This parable can be dangerous to Fives in the sense that they feel affirmed in not storing up physical things, which can be stolen, but they store up knowledge and information and hoard that instead. Their treasure is in their rich mental life, which cannot be stolen in the usual way.

The parable in action, the feeding of the five thousand, is more of a wake-up call to the Five's trance:

> Now when Jesus heard this, he withdrew from there in a boat to a lonely place apart. But when the crowds heard it, they followed him on foot from the towns. As he went ashore he saw a great throng; and he had compassion on them, and healed their sick. When it was evening, the disciples came to him and said, "This is a lonely place, and the day is now over; send the crowds away to go into the villages and buy food for themselves." Jesus said, "They need not go away; you give them something to eat." They said to him, "We have only five loaves here and two fish." And he said, "Bring them here to me." Then he ordered the crowds to sit down on the grass; and taking the five loaves and the

two fish he looked up to heaven, and blessed, and broke and gave the loaves to the disciples, and the disciples gave them to the crowds. And they all ate and were satisfied. And they took up twelve baskets full of the broken pieces left over. And those who ate were about five thousand men, besides women and children.

—Matthew 14:13–21

This parable is frequently presented as the multiplication of loaves with Jesus the hero creating more bread and fish. But Jesus himself refused to turn stones into bread back in Matthew 4:3. He did not come to furnish physical nourishment then or in this passage. A much better title for the parable would be "The Breaking of the Bread."

The first statement, "Now when he heard this," refers to the passage just before this parable. After hearing of John's beheading, Jesus went out into the wilderness to grieve. Like a type Five, he needed to be by himself in order to assimilate and deal with this tragedy within himself. But the crowds would not leave him alone. (Fives feel that way all the time—that too many demands are made on them.)

But Jesus is not allowed any time alone. It is significant that the way he handles his inner grief is by ministering to those who come to him. The disciples come off rather poorly, requesting that the multitudes be sent away (while they, too, have followed Jesus and would like to stay with the leader).

Matthew records that they fed five thousand, not counting women and children. They didn't count them because this was the standard way of estimating a crowd in those days: to count just the men and multiply by six. So thirty thousand people were probably fed that day out in a lonely place.

Most scholars agree that the real miracle is that Jesus persuaded people to share. Women never bring children on journeys without bringing food. And in this primitive pre-McDonald's era, people always carried food with them if they went any distance. So most likely what happened is that out of thousands of pockets and purses came their personal stash for the journey. Bread here, a Snickers bar there, figs—the usual portable fare.

So what happens is exactly contrary to the expectations and experience of the Five: people share and everyone gets enough. The shortage of sustenance, both physical and spiritual, is the perception that drives the type Five to hoard her time, energy, and affections. Fives assume that wealth will be depleted by others, the parable asserts that our individual poverty will be dissolved by the generosity of others. Fives are often willing to live solitary lives and even prefer it—like recluse billionaire Howard Hughes, a flaming Five—in exchange for those few things that make them feel rich.

Fives, like standard capitalists, define wealth as "what I have." The parable reframes wealth as "what we share." Entranced Fives have the same emotional stance as advanced capitalism: Whatever you have, I don't, and I either have to take yours or get along with as little as I can to make my meager wealth stretch as far as I can.

The emotional link between feeling poor and feeling isolated is very strong. A Five feels this most acutely, because he uses isolation for protection and, as he feels more and more isolated, he feels even poorer. His isolation is the source of his avarice. You can't give what you feel you don't have. Capitalism is Five writ large, and its enmity to community is the Five's sin desperately trying to remain out of sight. Capitalism has much going for it, but its basic premise is scarcity—the law of supply and demand. The theory is that in a world of scarcity, as supply decreases or demand increases, the price goes up correspondingly. Fives know scarcity in their fear-core, but Jesus says it isn't so.

The second miracle in the parable is that not only Jews, but people of every stripe were following Jesus. To get the Jews to share their kosher food and eat the unclean food, to share across economic, religious, and ethnic lines, is the kind of miracle that delineates the attitude of the kingdom. The miracle undoes the frightening world of threat and nonresponsiveness that the Five is used to living in. This kind of world makes his anti-social and highly protective trance unnecessary.

The parable is helpful to the Five believer because it reframes wealth and illustrates the mechanism by which community dissolves the inner fear that keeps the Five feeling poor and unable to share. Ultimately community cures avarice.

Like other parables, this one reveals the dynamics of the kingdom of God, in which there is plenty for everyone because people see themselves in community instead of competition.

Fives have some trouble with the first dynamic of kingdom behavior, the creation of community. When people live in community, they create an abundance; when they live in competition, they create the scarcity their struggle against each other is trying to solve.

In the Our Father, the request for bread is at the center of the axis of the structure of the prayer, and in the prayer, *bread* means whatever we need for life. The bread of the thirty thousand shares that symbolic richness; it is everything needed for the fullness of life that Jesus promised to bring.

As a trance, the belief that I don't have enough is usually oblivious to the resources that I have as an adult. A trance brings one's childhood trauma forward in time and controls behavior from that worldview. One way to understand trance is as an unblinking gaze at how poor and isolated one was as a young child. Entranced people live out the feelings and conviction of helplessness and hopelessness they experienced as small children. At some point a Five concluded that she was alone with her inner world and that what she had was *all* she had. Years later she lives off that memory and decides that what she had then is all she has now.

THE DYNAMIC

As with other Enneagram styles, the Five dynamic begins with a faulty belief that prompts him to give away what he spends so much energy trying to regain. In the Five, this seems to proceed something like this: His faulty worldview is that "People only take from you, they don't give." Once he has this early conviction, the rest of the script follows like water downhill. He can't get much if anything from people, so the best he can do is not let them drain off what meager resources he has. There's no more where this little bit came from, so he had better cherish what he has and learn to survive on as little as possible, with little interaction with people so he doesn't have to interact with being drained by these people. So given this shortage of goods, Five hoards what he can and isolates himself from people who would want his stash.

What the Five wants is the inner richness of emotional fullness, but she gave away her ability to request this because she "knew" her request would be denied. So now she spends all her efforts trying to meet her emotional needs by not sharing or reaching out. She meets her needs by setting her emotional carburetor extremely lean; she meets her needs for emotional richness by savoring in her head (like a miser gloating over money) what few emotional experiences she does have. She substitutes collecting things for direct and effective efforts to fill up her emotional longing. Her hoarding is compensatory, which is why it is done to excess. (Remember our principle of addiction: You never get enough of what you really don't want.)

Jesus tells a parable about a man who hoarded:

> He said to them, "Take heed, and beware of all covetousness; for a man's life does not consist in the abundance of his possessions." And he told them a parable, saying, "The land of a rich man brought forth plentifully; and he thought to himself, 'What shall I do, for I have nowhere to store my crops?' And he said, 'I will do this: I will pull down my barns, and build larger ones; and there I will store all my grain and my goods. And I will say to my soul, "Soul, you have ample goods laid for many years; take your ease, eat, drink, be merry."' But God said to him, 'Fool! This night your soul is required of you; and the things you have prepared, whose will they be? So is he who lays up treasure for himself, and is not rich toward God.'"

> **—Luke 12:15–21**

When Jesus describes the wealthy man, he describes the American capitalist with an adequate pension plan. "I've worked hard for thirty years and saved a few dollars, enough to live in modest comfort. I've earned my rest, now I'm going to travel and enjoy my retirement." Is there anything wrong with that?

Jesus is not giving financial advice. When he offers a parable, it is a parable of how life works following the principles of the kingdom. He tells us ahead of time, "Life doesn't consist of an abundance of possessions." But what does it consist of, then? This is an important question for the Five, because avarice does measure life by the equity in the giving/getting contract. Fives frequently live diminished lives out of that concern.

For Jesus, *life* is neither the technical traditional philosophical term, "self-moving" nor the dictionary definition, "the capability to take in food, turn it into energy, and adapt to an environment." For Jesus, the technical definition was an organic one: If you are united to God, you are alive, if you are separated from God, you are dead. This is the general biblical notion of life. Creatures live because they are in union with the Creator. Jesus gives his most eloquent expression of this in the parable of the vine and the branches. As long as we are united to God, we bear fruit because we are alive. And if we are cut off, we die.

The parable holds true in a psychodynamic sense also if you substitute the accumulation of possessions for the finer things in life: relationships, values, emotional richness, dedication to a higher cause.

The entranced Five can't see that accumulation is a substitution. Addictions substitute an inferior good for the real thing desired. In this case, it is life; Jesus brilliantly lays bare the contrast. So if the Five can assimilate this parable above, it will undo some of his distorted vision of life.

The parable owes some of its opacity to our secular mentality. Jesus assumes, as do many sensitive psychologists today, that everyone has a deep longing for a relationship with God. We fill up our lives with all sorts of substitutes to compensate for this relationship if it is missing. In the case of the Five, the compensation is greed for material things, as it is for the rich man in the parable. Jesus' whole issue with the rich in the Scripture seems to be rooted in his conviction that wealth subverted the longing for God. He states flatly at one point that we must serve either God or wealth:

No one can serve two masters; for either he will hate
the one and love the other, or he will be devoted to the
one and despise the other. You cannot serve God and
mammon.

—Matthew 6:24

What is clear in the sin of avarice and in the lives of Fives is that
wealth is a substitute for God. Life without God, without an
opening to infinity, is pinched and confining. The reason Jesus
would be against money, which is positive and necessary, is that
it is a substitute for our relationship with God. Any other interpretation of money runs into an anticreation attitude that Jesus
doesn't display anywhere. If God created wealth and all of the
things wealth brings, it can't be evil. The evil is that wealth can
displace our longing for God. The clue in the saying of Jesus is
the word "serve." Jesus is talking about total allegiance.

Once we are aware of that, the opening for grace becomes
wider. If we know we are searching for God as we count our
money, it changes our experience of counting. It makes the
counting a confession and opens us to the mystery of grace.

Describing Fives as emotional capitalists has some draw-
backs because the defense of a sensitive inner life is not connot-
ed, but the metaphor of capitalism works quite well if restricted
to the emotional exchange a Five envisions.

Fives are preoccupied with security, and capitalism balances
risk and security at all times. The language of "insurance," "secu-
rities," "Security and Exchange" and "securing loans" gives away
the underlying preoccupation. Capitalism is one articulation of
the theory of a worldview in which there is never enough.

The mystery of grace in the New Testament takes the opposite tack. In our relationship to God, we not only always have
enough, but we get it for nothing and we are obliged to share
with those to whom God is trying to give more. Our fundamental stance is not need, but gratitude for having our needs already
met, whether we realize it or not. Another parable gives an example of the dynamic of grace:

If you love those who love you, what credit is that to
you? For even sinners love those who love them. And if

you do good to those who do good to you, what credit is that to you? For even sinners do the same. And if you lend to those from whom you hope to receive, what credit is that to you? Even sinners lend to sinners, to receive as much again. But love your enemies, and do good, and lend, expecting nothing in return; and your reward will be great, and you will be sons of the Most High; for he is kind to the ungrateful and the selfish. Be merciful, even as your Father is merciful.

—Luke 6:32-36

The emotional capitalism of the Five is addressed by the fiscal metaphors of grace that Jesus uses. No capitalist or avaricious Five would lend without hope of repayment. The fullness of life envisioned here enables one to "not count the cost," and cost is another mercantile metaphor. Giving does deplete our substance, but only if we have a static and deprived view of ourselves. If we see giving as making room for more gifts from God, it is a drastically different experience. Fives see themselves as not having and not having been given. People, the external world in general, take rather than give. So whenever possible, a Five likewise does not give, because the expectation is that nobody will give back. That's why banks only loan money if they know they can take it back. The trust level in a fear-based person or system has to be kept as low as is possible to still engage in social and political activity.

The last parable I would suggest to Fives comes from several stories about Fives who left positions of security and went traveling around the world on little or no money. They did this, by their own telling, for their spiritual health. Taking inspiration from them, let's look at the movement in the following parable:

And a ruler asked him, "Good Teacher, what shall I do to inherit eternal life?" And Jesus said to him, "Why do you call me good? No one is good but God alone. You know the commandments: 'Do not commit adultery, Do not kill, Do not steal, Do not bear false witness, Honor your father and mother.'" and he said, "All these I have observed from my youth." And when Jesus heard it, he said to him, "One thing you still lack. Sell all that you have and distribute to the poor, and you will have treasure in heaven; and come, follow me." But when he heard this he became sad, for he was very rich. Jesus, looking at him said, "How hard it is for those who have riches to enter the kingdom of God! For it is easier for a camel to go through the eye of a needle than for a rich man to enter the kingdom of God."

—Luke 18:18-25

A Five has trouble entering into the flow of things. If she is deeply afraid of her environment and her usual strategy is to conserve what small (or large) quantities of time, energy, and money she does have, her great danger is a certain stagnation. Even fantasy has to be prompted by outside stimuli.

The rich man's position is a bit avaricious. He begins with flattery, "Good Teacher," about which Jesus immediately calls him to task. He wants to know how to gain eternal life. And he hopes to sweeten the answer with a little flattery, probably to get off as cheaply as possible.

Jesus really ups the ante. He says it will cost him everything. Love always requires that we put everything on the line. The kingdom, which plays by the rules of love, is no different. If he loves money (as the rich man's response will indicate), then of course total love requires him to give away his money. Had the man had power or beauty or some other currency he was clinging to, Jesus would have required that.

Ultimately, we don't need money for the kingdom. We don't need money to put ourselves at the service of God. Money is a hindrance because it requires a competing allegiance. We do things either for love or money.

The young man has to give up money in order to make room for love. The Five has to learn that: in order to enter into the flowing, exchanging, communal life of love, he needs to depend on love, not money. I explained earlier that the rules of money and love are opposed to each other. Money is the medium of exchange in the world of scarcity. Love is the medium of exchange in the world of abundance. We either live out of a perception of scarcity or out of abundance; we can't have it both ways. God or mammon.

WHAT CAN A FIVE DO?

1. Lift weights (whether you are male or female). Notice that you are organic. That means that the more effort you spend, the more strength you have. The emotional analogy is obvious, but learn the truth in your body, not just in your mind.

2. Put this sign on your desk (all Fives have desks): "You have to sing like you don't need the money."

3. Read the Gospel at one sitting. Notice the sense of abundance Jesus has in a variety of ways.

Sixes

SOME SENTRIES CARRY GUNS

Most of Jesus' parables of the kingdom of God reflect a world of fullness, of an abundance of love and earthly goods. The following parable is *not* a parable of the kingdom of God. It is a parable of how this wicked world works. Regardless of how many times it has been employed to encourage stewardship, a close examination will show that the nobleman who does the rewarding is not the God Jesus calls Father.

Notice the position in the Gospel. Luke positions it immediately before Jesus' entry into Jerusalem in triumph, fulfilling the crowd's expectations of how the messianic kingdom would come.

Before Jesus can make this messianic entrance, he has to correct the crowd's notion of messiah—and our notion of how God works. His disciples expected some kind of military, political triumph: Jesus' triumph will be conquering death, but they want him to conquer Romans. So in order to show them the dynamics of how the military–political victories come about and what kind of God it would take to make that system work, he tells them a parable about how earthly power is wielded:

> . . . he proceeded to tell a parable, because he was near
> to Jerusalem, and because they supposed that the
> kingdom of God was to appear immediately. He said
> therefore, "A nobleman went into a far country to
> receive kingly power and then return. Calling ten of

his servants, he gave them ten pounds, and said to them, 'Trade with these till I come.' But his citizens hated him and sent an embassy after him, saying, 'We do not want this man to reign over us.' When he returned, having received the kingly power, he commanded these servants, to whom he had given the money, to be called to him, that he might know what they had gained by trading. The first came before him, saying, 'Lord your pound has made ten pounds more.' And he said to him, 'Well done, good servant. Because you have been faithful in a very little, you shall have authority over ten cities.' And the second came, saying, 'Lord, your pound has made five pounds.': and he said to him, 'And you are to be over five cities.' Then another came, saying, 'Lord, here is your pound, which I kept laid away in a napkin; for I was afraid of you, because you are a severe man; you take up what you did not lay down, and reap what you did not sow.' He said to him, 'I will condemn you out of your own mouth, you wicked servant. You knew that I was a severe man, taking up what I did not lay down and reaping what I did not sow. Why then did you not put my money into the bank, and at my coming I should have collected it with interest?' And he said to those who stood by, 'Take the pound from him, and give it to him who has the ten pounds.' (And they said to him, 'Lord, he has ten pounds.') 'I tell you, that to every one who has will more be given; but from him who has not, even what he has will be taken away. But as for these enemies of mine, who did not want me to reign over them, bring them here and slay them before me.'" And when he had said this, he went on ahead, going up to Jerusalem.

—Luke 19:11–28

This is the God of the Six. This is how the world works under this God. It is antithetical to the kingdom of God portrayed in the other parables. Here there is no fullness, only fear, unfairness, and a system of rewards based on an arbitrary gift and an oppression of the poor and luckless. And the people hate him! The tradition of using this parable to get people to use their money wisely attests to our power to twist Scripture to fit our cultural needs. Once we have that image of God with those procedures in place, faith is not in our best interest! Why should we bare our sensitive soul to someone who slays his enemies and who "reaps what he did not sow," which means he takes more than he gives? A Six should read this parable, feel carefully for her deepest emotional reaction, and then be grateful that God is just the opposite of that.

The God of the Six is a frightening taskmaster whom he fears so much he is paralyzed. Sixes substitute worry for action and often are unable to take action, especially, as in this case, on their own behalf. When people see the allegory with the nobleman playing the role of God, they unblinkingly accept God as grasping (the meaning of "you take up what you did not lay down"), one whom nobody likes, one who rewards worldly success, and who slays his enemies. Quite a departure from the God who makes the lame walk, the blind see, and the poor receive the gospel. The nobleman fits the distorted view of God by Sixes, but it is not a parable of how God the Father operates.

This is not the same father who greeted the wayward son in the story often called the Prodigal Son. Contemporary scholarship prefers to title the parable, "The Prodigal Father," for it is the father who forgives all and throws a party. Quite a contrast with the grasping punishing figure in this parable. But these are the characteristics of authority, even divine authority, the Six entertains.

In order to understand faith, either in the Scripture or the Enneagram, we have to use a different definition than is used in popular culture, especially Catholic culture. In popular Catholicism, faith is agreement with what authority (pope, bishop, Scripture) says is true. "Do you believe that Jesus is the son of God?" Learning catechism answers feeds this understanding of faith. People make a big deal out of whether or not someone "believes" there is a God or believes what the church teaches.

That's not the biblical notion of faith, nor is it the Enneagram understanding. Faith is having a relationship to God and the universe that a loving God created.

God is Father (or Mother), and because that's the way God is, the universe is a good place to live in and make home. If we want to know our real image of God, complete the sentence, "The world is . . ." That sentence will tell us our faith issue.

Once we pray "Our Father, who art in heaven, thy will be done on earth as it is in heaven," we set up expectations of how God, heaven, and earth will treat *us*. It makes sense to ask for our daily bread. (You would never ask the nobleman in the parable for your daily bread.)

This is not a set of intellectual convictions. Some brilliant people believe, others don't. Faith is as much located in the muscles, the glands, and cellular processes as it is in the neo-cortex where the words of creed are formulated. Sixes, because they are head centered, get into special trouble when they try to get faith into their head. As soon as they try, their doubting mind begins to challenge what they are thinking.

Jesus describes a way of behaving that acts out the confidence that God is good and there is plenty to go around. He says:

> **. . . lend, expecting nothing in return and your reward will be great, and you will be sons of the Most High; for he is kind to the ungrateful and the selfish. Be merciful, even as your Father is merciful.**
>
> **—Luke 6:35**

Note the paradox of not expecting anything and yet being promised a reward. This paradox helps the Six because it frustrates the Six-based compulsion to "prove it." We have to let go in order to obtain. That's not logical, so it helps the Six get "out of her head." Sixes would do well to meditate on the contrast between this passage and the first parable. Ask the question, "What kind of context makes each passage make sense?" What kind of world is it in which we can give things away and not worry? And how does that differ from the parable of the nobleman who took away even what we did save? The important question is, "What kind of God created what kind of world?"

The sin of the Six is fear. Fear is usually considered an emotion, not a sin, but fear is a sin against faith. Sixes struggle against the power of fear. It oppresses them, as all sin does. The consequences of fear hurt, as they do in the parable above. The man who received only one pound just buried it. Sixes substitute thinking, especially worrying, for action. They fancy that in accomplishing something, they will incur the wrath of the authority. Inactivity is a way of lying low to escape that negative attention.

A metaphor for fear is the 'possum. The 'possum is not cunning. He does not lie down and pretend to be dead; he simply passes out from fear. This inadvertently protects him from predators who prefer their meals mobile. A Six I know, upon hearing that a high-level executive had been fired remarked, "The secret to longevity is a low profile so it doesn't occur to them to examine your work."

A certain number of Sixes are counterphobic. What they fear, they do. They prefer the "preemptive strike," in military terms. They would be 'possums with premium adrenaline that would attack the predator, even though it might be foolhardy.

The same worldview prevails in both cases, however. Both strategies try to cope with a hostile universe. Flight or fight are opposite reactions to the same perception.

Negative attention from the authority brakes their spontaneity because Sixes attend to authority. They may not like authority, but they seldom discount it. If a Six researcher were publishing, she would know what the authorities said. Then, and only then, might she take a stand to oppose them. But she would never, in the language of the pubescent, "blow them off" and publish without knowing where they stood, any more than as a child she would act without knowing where the parents stood, even while disobeying.

FAITH AND AUTHORITY

The relationship between faith and authority acts itself out both in the life of the Six and the actions of Jesus in the Gospels. Brother David Steindl-Rast (*We Dare to Say Our Father*, Credence Cassettes, 1993) argues that Jesus' approach to authority is revolutionary because of where Jesus located authority. Jesus had some choices about where to place authority. Being a prophet, he could have, as Isaiah, Jeremiah, and all the other prophets did, begun his discourse saying, "The word of the Lord came to me and said . . ." That phrase is on every other page of the Hebrew prophetical books.

Sometimes Jesus located authority within himself. "You have heard it said, but I say to you . . ."—a formula often used by charismatic leaders who are conscious of spiritual authority. (Chapter five of Matthew has a whole series of examples.)

But one of the more telling phrases Jesus used, especially on the Pharisees when they attacked him, was "Which of you?" For example:

> **Jesus spoke to the lawyers and Pharisees, saying, "Is it lawful to heal on the Sabbath, or not?" But they were silent. Then he took him and healed him, and let him go. And he said to them, "Which of you, having an ass or an ox that has fallen into a well, will not immediately pull him out on a Sabbath day?" And they could not reply to this.**
>
> **—Luke 14:3–6**

When Jesus' own authority is challenged, he appeals to the presence of the Holy Spirit within the Pharisees. Jesus knows that they are aware of what is right and wrong. And he knows that they know that they know! He trusts their authentic intuition, that Spirit within their hearts, and he knows that Spirit is the ultimate authority.

Sixes need to hear that address of Jesus. They need to acknowledge the presence of the Spirit within themselves in order to claim their inner authority. As long as authority remains external (and Sixes tend to love the military, the Church hierarchy, and political bureaucracy), the person is filled with fear.

FEAR VERSUS LOVE

Perfect love casts out fear. Perfect love is the Holy Spirit within us. Love casts out fear because it transfers authority from outside (where it can be used against one) to inside (where it is our deepest self).

A great deal of hand-wringing attention is paid to self-esteem in our schools, in self-help books, and on television

shows. Some of it is important. But techniques of self-esteem
don't heal like an integrated awareness that one has the Holy
Spirit within, so that one can decide for oneself the nuance, texture, and shape of one's destiny. A Six conscious of the inner
authority of the Holy Spirit has a powerful bulwark against fear-
ing external authority. Sixes do well to meditate on the presence
of the Holy Spirit within them.

Within the Six trance, the person gives away her power to
a hostile authority, then feels edible. It seems fitting that while
Jesus went around telling people their sins were forgiven so that
they were healed, one of his favorite miracles was healing the
lame so they could stand on their own two feet! Then he healed
the blind so they could see for themselves. Sixes could profit
from reading these healing miracles. They are images of grace
creating self-reliance based on faith.

Fear is as much a distortion of perception as any other
Enneagram sin. It is a particularly easy trance to support. If we
keep saying that bad things are going to happen, sooner or later
we are right. If a child wanders off in a shopping mall, ninety-
nine percent of the time people will make every effort to find the
parent(s). But one time in a hundred the child will be kidnapped.
Yet the fearful person will think it will happen every time, and
the one time it does happen it will make the news (which indicates it is not the norm) and the Six will say, "See, I told you,
that's what happens every time." Intermittent reinforcement of
their fearful worldview makes the Sixes' interior stance hard to
relinquish. The media custom of reporting only bad news is
toxic to Sixes. It confirms their worst fears. Sixes might abstain
from the evening news as a healthy discipline.

A Way Out

John's Gospel is chiastic. That means that the structure
is like a nest of parentheses (((()))): Chapter one goes with chapter twenty-one, chapter two with twenty, three with nineteen,
until you get to ten going with twelve, and chapter eleven standing
alone. It stands alone because it is the heart of the matter. It is
the story of Lazarus being raised from the dead. In the middle

of the story of Lazarus is the kernel of John's Gospel, John's key to everything:

> **I am the resurrection and the life, he who believes in me, though he die, yet shall he live, and whoever lives and believes in me shall never die. Do you believe this?**
>
> —John 11:25

Libraries of literature have been written on the layers of meaning in this statement. In order to live, you must go through death. To grow up you must not just get bigger, you must die to your childish ways. To get there, you have to leave here. This paradox is magic for the Six. The only way out is *through*. Six must take on the negative authority and endure whatever it takes to free oneself from its hold on her inner life. Only then can she break the trance, the memory of the power the authority used to have.

The centrality of this passage for the Six is clear. In order to conquer fear, one must trust a real (not just remembered) authority (Jesus), even to the extent of going through death. A little story captures a bit of the emotional truth. Jesus had strung a high wire over Niagara Falls and was going to ride his bicycle across it. He asked his disciples, "Do you believe I can ride across and back?" "Oh, yes," they replied, "you can do it." So he rode over and back. When he got back, the jubilant disciples reaffirmed their confidence. They were now absolutely positive and effusively told him so. He had proven it. So Jesus asked them again, "Do you think I can do it again?" This time they were even more confident and they assured him it was, in theological language, a piece of cake. "OK," he said, pointing to the handlebars, "Get on." The feeling we get when we think of getting on those handlebars relates to faith.

WHAT SIXES WANT

Sixes want faith. They want to live without fear. They want to know that "everything is going to be all right." They want what faith offers, an ultimate confidence that the universe is ordered and is a good place to live. They want to move about freely in a world a gracious God created for them. In a

Christian context, they want to live in a world in which death is overcome by life, dying is followed by rising. Living in faith is living in a universe that will ultimately care for you, one that is created out of love, to which you belong and in which you are welcome and comfortable. You call the Lord of the universe your parent, "Abba."

WHAT THEY SETTLE FOR

They settle for security. Security superficially resembles faith, but they are polar opposites. Living in search of security means living in a structurally hostile universe, one that will sooner or later get you. We talk of "security guards," "security measures," and a "national security state," which ultimately means living in a military climate. Security assumes measures against anxiety; faith doesn't have anxiety in the first place. Security is a tense accomplishment; faith is a relaxing gift.

At least twice, Jesus is tempted to choose security but chooses faith instead. The first time occurs after he has been baptized and is deciding his ministry. He goes out into the desert and is tempted to change stones into bread (Matthew 4:3). As mentioned earlier, bread in the wilderness was the sign that Yahweh had given the Israelites: They were allowed to take bread for only one day—no hoarding. Their act of faith had to be that the Lord would provide again the next day, so they were not allowed to provide for the next day. Jesus tells the tempter that his ministry is not going to provide bread; he will live by whatever God provides.

Again in the Garden of Gethsemani, he fears for his life, but rather than seek security (leaving the scene), he accepts whatever comes from his Father.

> **My Father, if it be possible, let this cup pass from me; nevertheless, not as I will, but as thou wilt.**
>
> —Matthew 26:39

The healing paradox for the Six is that when they can give up security, they can gain faith.

ADDICTION TO SECURITY

The paradox of relinquishing security follows the usual pattern of addiction. One must give up the short-term gain for the long-term one. The sin of fear alienates the Six from God because it refuses the risk of relationship. The inner path of refusal walks along these lines: Six is minding her own business when she sees something dangerous (on television, for example) that triggers memories of when she was small and edible. Rejecting reality (she is no longer edible), she defaults to an earlier position in her life (she was four and her father frightened her) and starts taking precautions so that what happened to those people on television doesn't happen to her. Each precaution reinforces her conviction about how dangerous the world really is and how scary her father was or is. She ends up more afraid. She takes as many precautionary measures as she feels are necessary to make her feel secure, at least for the time being. Then she is as secure as she was before she frightened herself.

Security and faith are opposed in the same way the inner and outer authority are opposed. Perhaps an analogy from biology would help. Concern about security moves one into a germ-free antiseptic environment. Faith relies on a healthy immune system. Notice the constriction that takes place when someone tries to be secure, and then notice the freedom of the person with a healthy immune system. Both strategies acknowledge danger, but security assumes helplessness and faith assumes inner power. That's the only sense in which fears are childish. The substitution of the outer for the inner is exactly the dynamic that weakens the Six. It is also the sin, that is, the false lookalike reality that is substituted for the real thing. In biblical terms, security is the idol that is worshipped.

How does Six achieve security in a dangerous world? First of all, he becomes wary, looking for the hidden dangers in chance comments, oblique observations, and circumstances that others don't notice or interpret. In order to do that, he has to maintain a high threshold of vigilance, to always be on the lookout. He doesn't trust easily, reads between the lines, and questions the smallest gesture. And since God is the most hidden and multi-interpreted presence in the world, Sixes have to check out God constantly. They check out everyone.

But, like all Enneagram trance addictions, that of the Six is a general interpretation of the world. If the cosmos is ultimately unfriendly and demanding, the only way to move in it is to test it frequently at first. This is why a Six is often called a devil's advocate. A lovely religious intuition realizes that not trusting is demonic. The demonic dynamic gets written large in our military. The military is a Six organization (that's why they call it defense department instead of the earlier term, war department). The other guys are bad, we're just defending ourselves. Colin Powell gave a speech to Congress in which he said, "The greatest enemy is the unknown enemy." He and the whole Six military are convinced in their souls that we do have enemies; it's just a matter of finding them. When Russia collapsed as evidence of mobilized hostility, the Pentagon immediately feared diffused hostility—we know they're out there, it's just that they haven't materialized yet. Now the national strategy is to have to be able to fight two wars at once. The trance tells Sixes that we need to be prepared and if one big enemy is gone, there are probably two smaller ones eager to take its place. If you suggested to them that no one in their right mind would attack us (and hasn't for fifty years), you would be added to the enemy list because you just don't understand how dangerous the world is. It is important not to be too cynical about the financial motives that underlie this conviction. The military system really believes that enemies are out there. They are not just lying to bloat the budget.

Security and fear depend on each other. The search for security begins as fear rises. One is only really inwardly secure when fear isn't an issue. But when fear is always an issue, security is always the purpose in life.

But what if God is the enemy (as the first parable indicated)? They suspect everything they perceive as coming from God. Problem: How do you ever check out God's real intentions?

The parables especially present an entirely different interpretation of the universe that has God present. For example:

One day he got into a boat with his disciples, and he said to them, "Let us go across to the other side of the lake." So they set out, and as they sailed he fell asleep. And a storm of wind came down on the lake, and they were filling with water, and were in danger. And they went and woke him say, "Master, Master, we are perishing!" And he awoke and rebuked the wind and the raging waves; and they ceased, and there was a calm. He said to them, "Where is your faith?" And they were afraid, and they marveled, saying to one another, "Who then is this, that he commands even wind and water, and they obey him?"

—Luke 8:22–25

Every Six knows that one should be afraid when the storms rage, but Jesus asks the ultimate question when he asks Sixes about their tumultuous universe: "Where is your faith? Where is your interpretation of events that can square up with the presence of God even in storms?" Sixes can profit from reading statements like these from Jesus, because they also have a strong connection to authority, and the very different authority of Jesus can be calming.

Later, right after Jesus has healed the woman with the hemorrhage on his way to heal the daughter of Jairus, Luke comments:

While he was still speaking, a man from the ruler's house came and said, "Your daughter is dead; do not trouble the Teacher any more." But Jesus, on hearing this, answered him, "Do not fear; only believe, and she shall be well."

—Luke 8:49-50

Going on experience, this is an unreasonable request. "Believe after death? I don't think so!" would be the usual reaction. But the message of hope for the Six is vivid: faith is life-giving. And of course, the Six has a lot of experience that security-addiction is death-dealing.

It becomes clearer that fear is not just a neutral emotional reaction, it is a life-stance that clings to a negative expectation of all reality, including God. It is the opposite of faith. After all, God and reality are pretty big compared to me and if they're all out to get me, of course I'm afraid. The negativity gets missed if we call fear just an emotion, because emotions are transient and reactions to current reality. Sin is systemic in the sense that it distorts our whole life-system.

One of the subtle ways for Sixes to undermine their fear is embedded in the Our Father and made explicit in the following parable in Matthew.

After Jesus is told that he is the son of God as he comes out of the waters of baptism, he is led out into the wilderness. There he is tempted. His first temptation, as cited above, is to turn stone into bread. Now bread is not just food: It is the symbol of life and is shorthand for all the good things that God gives us. Stone, on the other hand, symbolizes death and all the bad things of life. Jesus encourages us to trust God, to expect good things. He tells his disciples:

> **Ask and it will be given you; seek and you will find; knock, and it will be opened to you. For every one who asks receives, and he who seeks finds, and to him who knocks it will be opened. Or who of you, if his child asks for bread, will give him a stone?**
>
> **—Matthew 7:7–9**

In the temptation scene, Jesus is asked to turn the trials of life into the good things of life:

> **If you are the Son of God, command these stones to become loaves of bread.**
>
> **—Matthew 4:3**

but he answers from Deuteronomy 8:3:

> **Man shall not live by bread alone, but by every word that proceeds from the mouth of God.**
>
> **—Matthew 4:4**

In other words, we don't live by just the good things: We get life from everything that comes from God. "Word of God" here is the Word that created the heavens and earth in Genesis, it is not just information. It is the creative force behind all reality. Some of reality is pleasant, some is not, but it all comes from God, and as such it all gives us life. Jesus says he is willing to accept stones (i.e., death or any trial) if it comes from God, because it will be life-giving.

This is the attitude structured into the Our Father. The structure of the Our Father begins with the definition and name of God as "Abba," which is intimate and life-giving. Once you call God, "Abba," then you have every inclination to ask for bread. To expect bread, the good things of life from God, is precisely what the Six's interpretation of the world prohibits.

A touching example of how Jesus answers a doubting Six occurs in Chapter 11 of Matthew when John is in prison for speaking out against Herod. John acts just like a counterphobic Six. He does not want to be the leader. He says he is not even worthy to untie Jesus' sandals (John 1:9), and yet he has the impetuous courage to correct Herod to his face, an act of bravery and foolishness that would cost him his life. Now he is in prison and he begins to doubt: "Did I do this for nothing? Is Jesus really the Messiah?" So he sends his disciples to ask Jesus, "Are you he who is to come, or shall we look for another?" (Just like a Six: John has known Jesus since before both of them were born. He baptized Jesus; he knew about Jesus' activity; he said earlier he was not worthy to untie his shoelaces; he's been a loyal disciple. But he's got time to think in prison and the doubting mind gets the better of him. It's a little late for that question, but as a Six John probably had to ask it.) And Jesus answered them:

> **Go and tell John what you hear and see; the blind receive their sight and the lame walk, lepers are cleansed and the deaf hear, and the dead are raised up, and the poor have good news preached to them. And blessed is he who takes no offense at me.**

> **Matthew 11:4–6**

Jesus knows just how to reassure his disciple with the doubting mind. In the tradition, a self-proclaimed prophet was indistinguishable from an authentic prophet by word alone. So if Jesus were to say, "Yes, you're in luck, I am a true prophet and the Messiah," John would then have doubted Jesus' words as he was

already doubting his messianic identity. So Jesus (this is perfect
to reassure a Six) points to the authority of the tradition, to concrete (hard evidence) things that John can't deny but hasn't let
into his trance yet. The Messiah was to bring about just the things
that Jesus points to: John knows that tradition well. The combination of concrete evidence and the authority of the tradition is
enough to get by John's Six trance of the doubting attitude.

WHAT CAN A SIX DO?

1) To weaken the fear of authority, a Six could profitably read
any one of the synoptic Gospels and notice, memorize, and
absorb those passages (for example, Luke 5:17, 6:6, 11:37–
53, but there are many others) in which Jesus confronts the
oppressive authority (of both the Romans and the Pharisees)
with his own inner authority. His inner authority is your
inner authority—the presence of the Holy Spirit. And notice
that not only does Jesus appeal to the Holy Spirit within
himself, but within the Pharisees. And if the Pharisees, his
opponents, have the Holy Spirit, you can certainly count on
the presence of the Spirit within yourself.

2) Memorize the paradoxical statements that indicate dying in
order to live (John 11:25, Luke 9:23 or Matthew 10:34-39).
They don't make sense on a literal level and so they will get past
your conscious defenses and you can live out of the images.

3) Trances are repetitious reactions of childhood responses, so
they are literal. You feel just as afraid of the world now as if you
were three or seven years old. But because this is a literal
reproduction, this trance can be broken by parable and paradox. So memorize especially Matthew 7:7 and Luke 6:35. As
you do you will strengthen your faith. Matthew 7:7 and Luke
6:35 contain images of the universe that conflict with your
beliefs, so meditation on them will weaken your trance also.

4). Keep an image of an angel around. Angels appear 365 times
in scripture, one for every day of the year. Their opening line
is always "Be not afraid." Live with the image of an angel saying that to you every day and it will strengthen you.

Sevens

DENY EVERYTHING AND KEEP MOVING

Sevens are the optimists on the Enneagram. They are light-hearted, with enormous energy and a natural buoyancy that seems attractive to everyone, at least in the beginning. They move fast, love multiple options, are wide open to new ideas, new places, more and more exciting choices. They avoid being fenced in or shut down. They are naturally expansive, enthusiastic, and exciting. In short, theirs are the virtues of the young and young at heart. In fact, they are referred to in Enneagram literature as eternal children. (*Puer aeternus* or *puella aeterna* in classical literature).

The life of the court jester illustrates the Seven's fixation. The court jester, like the Seven, lives in terror. After all, if he is not funny or displeases the king, he loses his job and his head in one fell swoop.

The genius of the Seven is the genius of the court jester. Sevens are frequently gifted with words, diverting danger, even the king's wrath with charm. The Seven, the fool or jester, can tell the king things he needs to hear (that's her real job), but she has to tell him in such a way that he doesn't get angry. This tends to develop the skill of the Seven to tell the truth in a sweet and attractive way. Kings don't get the bitter truth, they get the sugar-coated version.

Now the art of telling the truth in a way that saves one's hide can easily turn one into a con man or charlatan. The Seven learns to entertain. Sevens believe that our two sayings about boredom—"bored to tears" and "bored to death" are real. Sevens flee boredom for themselves and try never to inflict it on others. They battle to keep terror at bay. Watch a comedian "die" for an illustration of the inner struggle of a Seven.

The Seven operates out of a vision of a deprived world. The world is seen as not being satisfying, so she tries to make it so. A Seven tells the story of coming home from a party with her slightly younger sister. When their mother asked them if they had a good time, the sister replied, "I don't know, Clara hasn't told the story yet." No party would be as good as her sister's telling of it.

WHAT DOES THE SEVEN WANT?

The Seven wants "satisfaction" in the literal meaning of that word—having enough. The Seven doesn't find satisfaction in what he is doing or having. His particular slice of reality lacks substance. Somewhere else, someone, something, is richer, more durable, more exciting. His slice is inadequate. He was dealt a poor hand and refuses to play it. Because he was dealt a weak hand, he will play another game, play by different rules, or play three hands at once.

WHAT DOES THE SEVEN SETTLE FOR?

Seven settles for more. If one party is boring, maybe having three lined up for the evening will ensure a good time. If one travel plan doesn't work out, maybe having backup plans B and C will make sure she gets there. If one lover is a bit doubtful, perhaps having two or three will guarantee emotional richness. Then again, they may not. Sevens unwittingly substitute quantity for quality and breadth for depth. Knowing how to play six musical instruments poorly isn't the same as playing one well, even if you spend about the same amount of time practicing.

THE MECHANISM OF IMPOVERISHMENT

How does the Seven impoverish the world so that he can then be forced to enrich it? Watch the high-speed, multi-option, cream-skimming approach. The Seven convinces himself that this reality, here and now, is dull. It is inadequate to yield pleasure and fulfillment. So picking over, he begins to create other options; if any plan lets him down, he can quickly switch places, companions, plans, clothes—whatever is necessary. A Seven is someone who has thirteen cheap suits and no good ones.

This variety ends up with a certain tedium. Seven realizes this tedium, so she solves it with the mechanism that got her into the problem in the first place. (We're lost, drive faster!) Eventually she may realize that she never gets enough of what she really doesn't want.

Sevens have a specific way of looking at the world that diminishes it. She looks only for the sunny side of life, so the world is flat and insubstantial. The weight of the darker side is missing and the Seven can suffer from a lack of gravity. Inappropriate joy becomes giddiness. Comic relief in a life filled with struggle is a delight. Continuous comedy is perpetual adolescence and is, ironically, ultimately boring. Carl Jung called the role of the court jester, the role of the Fool, an archetype. A court jester with nothing to say becomes a fool in the trivial sense of that word.

Because Sevens tend to look at the bright side of things, they feel little or no guilt. They skip from peak to peak in life, they don't trudge through the valley of darkness. They miss a lot by never going into the valley.

Jesus was tempted in the wilderness to opt for all good things and no bad ones:

> Jesus was led up by the Spirit into the wilderness to be tempted by the devil. And he fasted forty days and forty nights, and afterward he was hungry. And the tempter came and said to him, "If you are the Son of God, command these stones to become loaves of bread." But he answered, "It is written, 'Man shall not live by bread

alone, but by every word that proceeds from the mouth
of God.'"
—Matthew 4:1–4

Even though this response comes at the end of a fast, it is not primarily about food. The passage is probably shaped by the Our
Father (recorded later in Matthew) in which we ask for our daily
bread. We ask the Father for everything we need. We acknowledge that we are creatures and stand in total dependence. We live
by bread.

Stones, on the other hand, were death. In a later chapter,
Jesus says:

Or what man of you, if his son asks him for bread, will
give him a stone?
—Matthew 7:9

Jesus refuses to live by only the good things of God, he insists that
he will live by every word of God. He will accept the negative and
the positive, he will accept both death and life from his father.

This is precisely the dynamic the Seven must learn—the
fullness of life comes through a dying and rising. To bypass
death is to be forever frivolous, wondering why reality doesn't
satisfy. To refuse the stones is to refuse part of reality. The sin of
gluttony is the dynamic solution to the problem of living without the full range of human experience that includes death. It's
like listening to music on a stereo with the bass speakers shot.
The music doesn't satisfy, even if the volume is turned up. Some
heaviness is essential.

THE INDEPENDENT PRODIGAL

The story of the Prodigal Son in Luke 15:11–33 is especially helpful for Sevens, but for reasons not immediately apparent. In many scenarios, Sevens gave up on authority as children.
They often are forced to grow up too fast and be their own parents and have as an inner motto that it is never too late for a
happy childhood. Because of this, they are frequently called the
most "self-referential" of all the numbers.

The dynamism of the prodigal father story has the son wanting to be self-referential. He was probably living a fairly good life at home, but he wanted, in today's terms, to be "independently wealthy."

The desire to be *independently* wealthy corrupts one and goes against the mainstream of biblical thought. The biblical concept is that we are *dependently* wealthy. Our Father, who knows what we really need, will give us everything we need—daily. We are wealthy because we are connected. We are wealthy because Our Father owns the world. We are wealthy beyond our fondest dreams because we have been given a planet of unutterable beauty and richness. But we are creatures. Jesus will develop at great length the theme of the vine and the branches in John's Gospel. His central message will be that we will flourish only to the extent we are in union with him as he is with his father.

The prodigal son does not know that wealth consists in being united with his father. He wants to be disconnected. The son eats the food of pigs, an abomination to Jews. He profoundly insults his father because asking for his inheritance was the equivalent to telling his father he wanted him dead. And the only thing the young man had to gain was to have his wealth without connection to his father.

Sevens need to realize that the Father never breaks the connection. Sevens appear to accomplish this easily, because they don't feel much guilt. They don't see why God wouldn't be united with them. But, like the prodigal son, when pain and failure hit, it is difficult for a Seven to appreciate the presence of God, because Sevens see pain as something to be avoided. If God is not creating a pleasurable world, God is not really doing what God is supposed to. Or God does not exist in any meaningful way and is certainly not on his side.

The point of the father's rejoicing is that the son was dead and now has come back to life. In biblical thought, life and union were almost synonymous. Agricultural people know that if a branch or flower or root is severed, it dies. People do, too. Sevens don't always see that clearly. Their relationships tend to be superficial and frequently not life-giving. Going through death to reach newer stronger life is precisely what Sevens do poorly.

Sevens should read that parable as a declaration of dependence and see in the prodigal son the sin of independence. Our individualistic culture only encourages the Seven's independence, so the Gospel story is a good corrective image.

LOST AND FOUND

Jesus says:

> What woman, having ten silver coins, if she loses one coin, does not light a lamp and sweep the house and seek diligently until she finds it? And when she has found it, she calls together her friends and neighbors, saying, "Rejoice with me, for I have found the coin which I had lost." Just so, I tell you, there is joy before the angels of God over one sinner who repents.
>
> —Luke 15:8–10

A world of difference prevails between being righteous and repenting. The behavior might be identical. The genius of the Enneagram concerns itself about the flow of energy rather than surface behavior. And while Jesus was flexible about the behavior of his followers, he was insistent that they repent, as were John before him and the prophets before them.

Luke precedes this parable with another one making the same point:

> What man of you, having a hundred sheep, if he has lost one of them, does not leave the ninety-nine in the wilderness, and go after the one which is lost, until he finds it? And when he has found it, he lays it on his shoulders, rejoicing. And when he comes home, he calls together his friends and his neighbors, saying to them, "Rejoice with me, for I have found my sheep which was lost." Just so, I tell you, there will be more joy in heaven over one sinner who repents than over ninety-nine righteous persons who need no repentance.
>
> —Luke 15:3-7

Matthew uses the parable to obliterate the distinction between good and bad people, as mentioned earlier, but Luke uses it to exalt the dynamism of repentance. Jesus is not giving advice. Like all parables, when taken literally, this one boggles the mind, as it is supposed to do. That's why parables keep spiraling down into our depths and dissolve the patterns of the childish thought that keep us living in an impoverished world. Our Enneagram trance, focusing on only a few remembered realities, keeps us rigid, defensive, and ashamed. The parables break down our distorted images and convince us we are wrong. Then we are free to consider the invitation of God.

Sevens find repentance repugnant in a way specific to them. Repentance means facing the subconscious material. It means acknowledging that some things are not fun and lighthearted. Repentance is the movement from safety and pleasure down through corruption and unfamiliarity to something that is not well defined on the other side. All heroes are edible, and in the beginning of all stories, things don't go well in the kingdom. Sevens are not convinced of the necessity of facing the bad times, so when Jesus values repentance more than staying good, he says something that doesn't make immediate sense to Sevens—and is therefore enormously valuable to them.

The parable deliberately frustrates. Why should one be rewarded more for making the transition from bad to good than for staying good? Why should one rejoice so much over finding what was lost rather than not losing something? One can understand a human emotional surge at finding what was lost, but it seems strange for God to do that.

The message is deeper. Spiritual growth comes from assimilating the negative. The contribution of the Enneagram is that it articulates the negative that needs to be assimilated. The parable insinuates this truth into imagery that will remove the mask of gaiety of the entranced Seven.

The story of the prodigal contains a hidden danger for the Seven. Sevens are often seductive and one way they seduce people is by being forgiving themselves. Because they are cheerfully anti-authoritarian and a bit casual about law and convention, they can find it easy to make friends with the vices of their friends. Sevens can forgive the destructive or immoral behavior (as long as it doesn't affect the Seven, of course). So if the Seven identifies with the prodigal father (as a parent might), she might make sure she forgives people who really offended her, not just those who broke a law or violated a convention.

THE JOY OF REPENTANCE

Because Sevens are optimistic and animated, people assume they are happy. They're no happier than any other number. They just truck only with the happy part of life. They deny the remainder. They move quickly over the shadowy side of life, but they know exactly where it is, if only to avoid it. Repentance is the only way to authentic happiness—but it is dark and painful.

Unhealthy Sevens don't consciously suffer as much pain as they inflict. Outside reality often has to restrain them. In the prodigal parable, the son "came to himself," but he was a little like a Seven in that he didn't come to himself until he ran out of money, friends, and food. A vigilant type Six, for example, may have noticed when the money was ten percent gone that this behavior could only go on for so long. Sevens are specialists in not noticing until the pig food starts looking good.

ACCENTUATE THE NEGATIVE

Even though Jesus presents parables of the fullness of life that are extremely attractive to the Sevens, he presents a number of sayings that dismantle the emotional world-structure of the Sevens, including this series of sayings that a Seven should assimilate:

> He began to teach them that the Son of man must suffer many things, and be rejected by the elders and the chief priests and the scribes, and be killed, and after three days rise again. And he said this plainly. And Peter took him, and began to rebuke him. But turning and seeing his disciples, he rebuked Peter, and said, "Get behind me, Satan! For you are not on the side of God, but of men."
>
> —Mark 8:31–33

An unhealthy Seven behaves much like a false prophet. She tells the authority only what will please them. Peter goes even further in the Gospel of Matthew: He won't let Jesus talk about the death that he must face:

> From that time Jesus began to show his disciples that he must go to Jerusalem and suffer many things from the elders and chief priests and scribes and be killed, and on the third day be raised. And Peter took him and began to rebuke him, saying, "God forbid, Lord! This shall never happen to you." But he turned and said to Peter, "Get behind me, Satan! You are a hindrance to me; for you are not on the side of God, but of men."
>
> —Matthew 16:21–23

The Seven trance of compulsive optimism can be weakened by the fundamental dynamic of Jesus' life: He conquered death by dying; he defeated the power of evil by letting it kill him. When a Seven absorbs this, the paradoxical structure gives her courage to face layers of death in her life.

Another parable can help Sevens:

> If any one comes to me and does not hate his own father and mother and wife and children and brothers and sisters, yes, and even his own life, he cannot be my disciple. Whoever does not bear his own cross and come after me cannot be my disciple. For which of you desiring to build a tower, does not first sit down and count the cost, whether he has enough to complete it? Otherwise, when he has laid a foundation, and is not able to finish, all who see it begin to mock him, saying, "This man began to build and was not able to finish."
>
> —Luke 14:26–31

Jesus asks for total commitment. Hating one's relatives must be understood against the background of an identification of religion and ethnicity. For the Jews, all other peoples were unclean. The special word, *Gentile*, is a term of scorn. Certain foods, certain animals were unclean and so were certain people. To consider all people children of God—Jesus' major theological achievement—was beyond most Jews of Jesus' time. Loving all people as children of God would certainly offend family and relatives and cause enmity. Jesus' point was that the commitment to this universal parenthood and universal sister/brotherhood was so important that it must stand against all other attachments. The saying underlines the painful darker side of love—it may cost you everything—so it challenges the worldview of the Seven.

COMMITMENT AS CONFINEMENT

Sevens keep total commitment at bay. It feels like confinement. They prefer multiple options, doing three things at once with temporary and relative commitment. The multiple options defend against the feeling of not being able to count on any of them. When that defense is applied to relationships, multiple relationships mean neither side should rely on total commitment. Jesus requires the opposite.

The Sevens' lack of commitment goes to their core fear style. They get into trouble when they absent themselves from bonding, but the motivation is distrust, not rejection. They can't rely on the other person, so they develop a backup. Sevens live in an unreliable world. That is how fear opposes faith. Jesus says you can count on God, even if you lose your life. Fear says not only can't we count on God: we can't count on anybody or anything much.

So Jesus says:

Whoever of you does not renounce all that he has cannot be my disciple.

—Luke 14:33

Renunciation is very difficult for a Seven because it's like asking a person who customarily builds bridges out of five layers of dubious timbers to give up that comforting bulk to cross the river on only one timber. It will take a lot of assurance to get Seven out on that single thickness.

What Jesus does to get the Seven out on the bridge is convince him, by use of paradox, that his current bridge won't hold:

He who finds his life will lose it, and he who loses his life for my sake will find it.
—Matthew 10:39

The paradox neutralizes the fear of loss by addressing it head-on: If you try to take care of your needs with your own power, if you try to succeed, if you try to "make something of yourself," you are doomed to failure. Seven knows this makes sense. Because she can't trust any one person, place, or activity to fulfill her, she keeps flitting. So that part of the paradox hooks her. If she's going to die anyway; if this bridge or that limb, this person or that job is going to prove unreliable, then give it up. Trust what can't be trusted because it's the only game in town. This happens to many Sevens. They come for therapy out of exhaustion or because their family insists that their life isn't working.

But when one reduces a paradox or parable to a rational explanation (and never forget, it is a radical reduction), something crucial is lost. A paradox is a dynamic imbalance. Every time it shows up in our consciousness, we have a new context, a new facet, a new understanding. Losing one's life to gain it means disequilibrium in a slightly different way every time one approaches it.

This disequilibrium is the source of growth, like the decay of last year's leaves is the food for this year's plant. The lost and found parables illustrate that nicely. Why would Jesus prefer the parables of lost and found to parables of never having been lost? Why not have an undefeated season? Why not tell parables of staying found, with instructions on how not to get lost? The spiritual life is one of constant growth and improvement. That means going where you haven't gone before, which in turn is a type of being lost.

Sevens are often well-behaved for just this reason. Sevens lead with charm and part of charm is doing what pleases everyone; they don't lose themselves. They often stay in the good graces of everyone, at least until things get unpleasant. But of course, Sevens try to avoid having that happen.

Real morality involves decisions that make one unpopular at times. Real morality doesn't have a clear map; it is too textured and nuanced to have a rule book. So Sevens often play by the rules so as to avoid unpleasantness and pain. That makes for good behavior, but it is not Christian morality.

THE DREADED CROSS

The most comprehensive paradox was used by Jesus to frustrate the Seven's energetic search for a life of thornless roses:

If any man would come after me, let him deny himself and take up his cross and follow me. For whoever would save his life will lose it; and whoever loses his life for my sake and the gospel's will save it. For what does it profit a man, to gain the whole world and forfeit his life? For what can a man give in return for his life?

—Mark 8:34–37

Here Jesus raises the ante in a way that boggles the mind. Life is at stake. He says that we can gain the whole world—probably attractive to a type whose major sin is gluttony. But after we gain the whole world, we lose.

The question Jesus raises and doesn't answer is why should gaining the whole world cost us our life? He assumes the answer or he assumes his listeners know the answer. In this place in Mark's Gospel—of course, the Evangelist means it very concretely—Jesus is on his way to Jerusalem and he will lose his life and his disciples will do likewise if they are faithful.

But that just pushes the question deeper. Why did Jesus voluntarily die? Christian tradition carefully distinguishes his actions from suicide, because he died for a cause, his gospel.

That may give us some insight into the psychological dynamics that are so hard for a Seven to grasp. When we consider any one thing so important that we will die for it, we gain our life. It is, unlike much frivolous pleasure, satisfying. You've seen people, even with an ignoble cause like white supremacy or a trivial cause like a football team, alive with fire and enthusiasm. Their vitality and cause may be trivial, but the dynamics are real. Commitment releases energy by its focus. Jesus considered his gospel so important he was entirely willing to die for it. His understanding of the Father's relationship to the world was so important, so central, and so life-giving that even his own death should not stand in the way of people's knowing of it.

The glutton, always flitting, always taking, needs to learn the dynamic of letting go, and letting go on a number of levels. The fearful glutton has the psychological equivalent of obesity. The glutton can't say no to anything, until forced into a diet in which he has to say no to almost everything to "save his life." But it isn't an indiscriminate letting go. It has to be preceded by the commitment, and commitment is always an act of faith.

The paradox forces movement within the Seven. The combination of threatening her with death (losing her life) which addresses the fear and the promise of new life (which hooks the gluttony) puts the Seven into a state of perpetual motion, like the negative and positive poles of an electromagnetic armature in a motor. In order to get what she wants the most, she will have to do what she wants the least. So fear and desire, her two controlling passions, are pitted against each other. Neither one will ever go away, so no matter how much she wants or fears, she is constantly having to deal with both of them. To the extent she believes there is life after pain and death, to that extent she will be able to face them. And to the extent she is willing to face them, she is rewarded by what she wants most—the fullness of life.

WHAT'S A SEVEN TO DO?

An ancient Christian tradition pictured the cross with jewels on it and without any corpus or body of Christ on it. In Latin, the *crux gemnata*. For Sevens, it contains the promise of glory within suffering. Keep it someplace important.

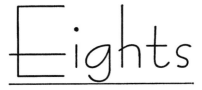

Eights

THE AFFECTIONATE TANK

I f you have a big job to do, or a tough battle to fight, or you need a fierce friend when times are tough, look for an Eight. When Eights are healthy, they are among the most vital, energetic, accomplishment-oriented, and festive comrades you could have. They can be fearless and tireless with the ideals of a Knight of the Round Table.

Healthy Eights make fine friends and truly superlative leaders. They can make decisions, operate from a position of strength, and have the energy and courage to do what has to be done, regardless of personal cost.

Healthy Eights are able to synthesize two apparent opposites: fierceness and gentleness. They will take on any foe if the cause is just, and if you are the victim of an unjust situation, you can count on a healthy Eight all the way home. Heroism is their energy for mercy, against injustice.

Eights tend to experience life as a combat zone, so they focus on the issue of power, as a warrior looks at opponents to measure their strength in case of an attack. Eights personify what we would consider the good and the bad points of a soldier or warrior: powerful, self-denying, loyal to his group and destructive of the "others," single-minded, resourceful, and suffused with a fierceness that has been instilled to make him a fighting machine.

The intensity of the Eight is called lust by most in the Enneagram tradition. Lust in the medieval scholastic tradition of

St. Thomas was only about sex, but in the Enneagram tradition it indicates a generalized intensity— a lust for life. Eights are prone to excess in food, drink, work, sex, and play—and, while partying, volume and duration.

WHAT EIGHTS WANT

Eights want justice. They perceive their early life as having been unfair or a time of abuse. They are determined that this injustice must stop. Stopping injustice isn't the same as establishing justice, but the healthier one is, the closer these ideals mesh. Redeemed Eights are often in the forefront of social action, especially on behalf of those who cannot obtain justice for themselves: the sick, the young, the elderly, or the culturally disadvantaged. More often than not, the social action group of the parish is headed up by an Eight. Eights are gut types, with anger for their motivation. When they see injustice, their instinctive and powerful reaction is to redress the situation. The more physical and public the injustice, the quicker and more powerful the Eight's reaction. She is more determined than diplomatic, and her default position is the belief that the best way to search for justice is to use power— not necessarily force, although that's an attractive option as well.

WHAT THEY SETTLE FOR

Revenge. Eights are acutely aware of the injustices in the world, having suffered these themselves. So they are going to do unto others before others do unto them. Pardoxically, Eights are so intent on this redress that they are prone to bully people and be highly unjust, while in their mind they are simply restoring balance. Some Eights have a chip on their shoulder; most don't. Many times, under stress, they withdraw and are silent until someone attacks them—then they go into action. Many of the taciturn cowboys in the old western movies played Eights: they believed in redemptive violence. Many teachers call the Eights "avengers," and many Eights come from a background of real or perceived injustice. Their anger is an armored resolution not to let the world inflict that injustice on them any longer.

The more unhealthy the Eight, the more their activities are a gut reaction to something wrong rather than a reasoned and balanced establishment of justice. They are addicted to the pleasure of revenge. Revenge is momentarily satisfying, but it does not create justice. It usually creates an imbalance in Eight's favor and that feels good for the time being, but it is not justice. Worse, it reinforces his sense that the world is a hostile place wherein he has to eat or be eaten.

What the Eight finally wants is nurturing, or *emotional* justice. Nurture is missing in her experience. Because she values it and can't obtain it, she frequently projects her need onto others and takes care of them instead.

Like all addicts, Eights never get enough of what they really don't want. Eights really do want a kind of cosmic justice, but they are addicted to revenge instead. When they rightly seek justice on a real emotional level, they look for nurture, which creates inner equilibrium; revenge, on the other hand, just rearranges the arrows of ache.

Revenge doesn't work. It doesn't heal the injustice experienced as a child. An Eight still feels those hurts. But how can an adult punish her parent/teacher/coach—whoever it was that she feels treated her unjustly as a child? And even if she could, it wouldn't make an Eight feel any better for any length of time. Emotionally, revenge isn't possible. Whatever the Eight lost as a child, she can't get back as an adult.

Besides childhood injustice, even current injustices can't be redressed. One can't bring back a lost name, a betrayed friendship, a broken vase or even a hurt feeling. Courts try to quantify things with money but that doesn't work well either.

The Eight trance that flows from this worldview is a constant narrowing of attention to decide whether a person is a friend or foe. Entranced Eights tend to view all relationships in terms of black and white; they see their enemies as cartoons or caricatures. Rush Limbaugh displays his Eight trance frequently. One night on "The Late Show with David Letterman" he said that Hillary Clinton (one of his favorite enemies) looked like a hood ornament on a Pontiac. He really sees her that way: no nuances, no texture, not somebody with good and bad points, just a cartoon figure without dimension. This trance is necessary to attack someone. In war, soldiers have to dehumanize the enemy if they're going to kill with any enthusiasm. Soldiers make the enemy into a cipher or caricature: "Gooks," "slopes," "krauts," call them anything but human— the list is as long as military history. What is public when nations fight each other is private and inward in the trance of an Eight, who is ready for war at any time.

GOOD WEEDS

Jesus' next parable has the kind of worldview that understands the *mixture* of good and evil in both Rush Limbaugh and Hillary Clinton that Eights have a difficult time assimilating.

> The kingdom of heaven may be compared to a man who sowed good seed in his field, but while men were sleeping, his enemy came and sowed weeds among the wheat, and went away. So when the plants came up and bore grain, then the weeds appeared also. And the servants of the householder came and said to him, "Sir, did you not sow good seed in your field? How then has it weeds?" He said to them, "An enemy has done this." The servants said to him, "Then do you want us to go and gather them?" But he said, "No; lest in gathering the weeds you root up the wheat along with them. Let both grow together until the harvest; and at harvest time, I will tell the reapers, 'Gather the weeds first and bind them in bundles to be burned, but gather the wheat into my barn.'"

> —Matthew 13:24-30

This brilliant parable is about the mixture of good and evil and the proper way to deal with it. Eights have to resist the forcible extraction of what is evil. Revenge rips out the evil and annihilates the evil ones. When Eights do that, they destroy as much as they correct. This parable can be applied intrapersonally, also: We can't even forcibly root out our own faults without destroying our good qualities. Every Enneagram student should meditate on this parable when he or she tries to deal with the chief fault of his or her number.

Sporting events and wars are dedicated to opposing the genius of this parable. Wars turn the other country into demonic enemies that richly deserve to be nuked. The United States is still angry because "we" didn't get to kill Sadam Hussein. Sporting events likewise divide the world neatly into good and bad. Whatever bad happens to them is good for us, and vice versa. But when that sporting or military metaphor is exported off the playing or battlefield, it is profoundly limited and destructive. The black/white, either/or thinking that is necessary for victory in sports and war doesn't begin to describe complex reality where goodness and evil grow together in the same person, country, or event. Jesus' parable is a powerful antidote to that kind of toggle-switch, good/bad thinking.

One reason war, sports, and old-fashioned western movies are attractive is that they seem to solve the stress of complexity. But if John Wayne had had to deal with the Indian children the next morning, he might have tried something other than gunfire.

GOOD SAMARITAN: OXYMORON?

The parable of the Good Samaritan illustrates the Eight's dilemma. You know the story:

And behold, a lawyer, stood up to put him to the test, saying, "Teacher, what shall I do to inherit eternal life?" He said to him, "What is written in the law? How do you read?" And he answered "You shall love the Lord your God with all your heart, and with all your soul, and with all your strength, and with all your mind; and your neighbor as yourself." And he said to him, "You have answered; do this, and you will live." But he, desiring to justify himself, said to Jesus, "And who is my neighbor?" Jesus replied, "A man was going down from Jerusalem to Jericho, and he fell among robbers, who stripped him and beat him, and departed, leaving him half dead. Now by chance a priest was going down that road; and when he saw him he passed by on the other side. So likewise a Levite, when he came to the place and saw him, passed by on the other side. But a Samaritan, as he journeyed, came to where he was; and when he saw him, he had compassion, and went to him and bound up his wounds, pouring on oil and wine; when he set him on his own beast and brought him to an inn, and took care of him. And the next day he took out two denarii and gave them to the innkeeper, saying, 'Take care of him; and whatever more you spend, I will repay you when I come back.' Which of these three, do you think, proved neighbor to the man who fell among the robbers?" He said, "The one who showed mercy on him." And Jesus said to him, "Go and do likewise."

—Luke 10:25–37

Jews hated Samaritans. The lawyer, like the Eight, divided the world into good guys and bad guys, Jews (neighbors) and Samaritans (aliens). Jesus confounds the lawyer—and the typical Eight—by seeing the good in the bad guys. In sports and the military, uniforms are worn so we can always tell who is good and who is bad—whom to shoot or tackle. In real life, bad guys don't wear uniforms. Worse yet, whoever is good today may be bad tomorrow. Or whoever is good in one way may be bad in another. The lawyer is wrong about the way he sees the world. So are Eights. They are both wrong in the same way, dividing it up neatly into teams. The point of the parable is *not* that you should take care of people in distress; the lawyer already knew that. The point is that nobody is all good or all bad. When coaches proclaim that football is more than a game, it is a metaphor for life, they do a great deal of harm. If good guy/bad guy game thinking creeps into life as well, it can create havoc or Bosnia. Eights are particularly vulnerable to this. They need to absorb the parable.

All types have power. Eights are concerned about external, active, coercive power. They aren't interested in the power of music or the power of persuasion. They prefer their power physical, sensate, and external. They're frequently big strong people, especially through the shoulders. Physical power works better for people built like that. At the onset of conflict, the Eight experiences a rush of pleasure where others might feel pain. It could be compared to the taste of jalapeno peppers. For many of us, the bite is so strong it causes acute pain. But if one is accustomed to the sharp bite and is addicted to capsicin (the active chemical), then the experience is pleasure. It makes one feel alive! Eights experience an analogous rush of vitality in conflict.

The reason that Eights enjoy conflict is simple and sad. It confirms their worldview. It tells them they are right. The world is a place in which people are not fair and are out to get you if you don't get them first. "It's a tough world; it's a good thing I'm so strong." If this seems incomprehensible, watch a football game any Saturday afternoon and note the pleasure people derive from the experience of physical combat. And boxer Mike Tyson is rich because he gives audiences a vicarious thrill by beating people up.

Eights can be lonely. They are frequently cynical about other people's virtue and benevolence. Their worldview is competitive; they imagine that everyone is against everyone. That makes it hard for them to see themselves as part of any group they don't control. It can be lonely at the top, and that's the only place they're comfortable.

THE CONQUEROR

Jesus lived in what appears to be a rather Eight-based culture. Material poverty, singular religious views, and oppression by foreigners in their history had given the Jews ample reason to view the world as a hostile place that had to be conquered. They longed for kings to avenge them, and above all they longed for a messiah who would avenge them. When Jesus showed messianic promise, each group read him as their divine champion, as the warrior who would free them.

So Jesus uses a number of stories and symbolic actions to disabuse them of their military expectations; the greatest such symbol, of course, was the cross. But long before that, he rejected their political and military opinions with parables and symbolic actions.

One of the delightful symbols he used to "reframe" their expectations of a conquering Messiah was the donkey he rode into Jerusalem. As he rides in everybody shouts "Hosannah" and gives him a Messiah's welcome. But he's not riding a white horse! He's not in a chariot with mighty steeds. He's riding an ass, and a colt at that. Why? As if to say, "Yes, I am your Messiah, I will do the expected conquering march into town with the crowd cheering. I will lead you, but notice my warhorse!" His different warhorse leads a different parade because he is going to be a different Messiah than they expected.[1]

Mark's account notes that the young ass had never been ridden before. How could one tell? It seems that "never been ridden" means that there had never been a ride like this; this is going to be a brand new kind of victory march. The warhorse must not have gotten used to the old way of being in battle, because he was going to do something brand new. I suggest that Eights keep a statue of an ass around, just for meditation. It's a tough little animal, but it has a certain reserve and modesty that healthy Eights wear well.

Before going to more parables, let's look at another of Jesus' injunctions, because it comes from a worldview radically different from that of an Eight. The text reads :

Ask, and it will be given you; seek, and you will find; knock, and it will be opened to you. For every one who asks receives, and he who seeks finds, and to him who knocks it will be opened.

—Matthew 7:7–8

The Eight trance sees a much different world. His world is one in which you have to do it yourself. Asking feels like a form of weakness and it has been Eight's repeated early experience that if she wants a door opened, she should knock hard, and if that doesn't work, she'll simply knock it down. Jesus suggests an infinite graciousness and a nurturing relationship to his Father that Eights need but find hard to accept.

---

1. This interpretation of the passion narrative in Mark's gospel is taken from Eugene LaVerdiere's video cassette program, *The Gospel of Mark* (Credence Cassettes, 1994).

Eights see God's world as unsupportive, not nourishing. Jesus tries to tell us that our Father knows what we need and is eager to give it to us. Many Eights have trouble with petitionary prayer and report frequent anger and rage against God. They have trouble reconciling the injustice they feel with the justice they feel God should be creating in the world. To their credit, they're often willing to help with that justice.

THE NATURE OF LEADERSHIP

Right after the mother of the sons of Zebedee had asked if they could have the places of honor, Jesus replied:

> **You know that the rulers of the Gentiles lord it over them, and their great men exercise authority over them. It shall not be so among you; but whoever would be great among you must be your servant, and whoever would be first among you must be your slave; even as the Son of man came not to be served but to serve, and to give his life as a ransom for many.**
> **—Matthew 20:25–28**

This reframing of leadership puts the Eight in a quandary. Eights are natural leaders, taking charge by virtue of their energy and focus. How does one take charge by washing feet or waiting tables or calming children?

The servant/leadership paradox can be particularly helpful to Eights. Healthy Eights can serve the weak. To do that they have to realize that combat is a way of feeling more alive. If they can nurture their inner life with feelings of compassion for the victims of injustice, they will feel less alone and will see less need to fight to avenge themselves. They serve the defenseless. They remain warriors, but they become knights defending what is holy. They understand well that little people serve big people and big people serve little people but all people serve some people. Entranced Eights determine to serve no one because of their convction that no one is on their side. But even if that's the case, they can maneuver and be on somebody else's side. There's nothing wimpy about that, if it is clear that they don't need anything from the others. And of course, if they are serving the needy and helpless, that is true. They serve well.

Another powerful parable, known by everyone, is frequently misunderstood:

> **You have heard that it was said, "An eye for an eye and a tooth for a tooth." But I say to you, "Do not resist one who is evil. But if any one strikes you on the right cheek, turn to him the other also; and if any one would sue you and take your coat, let him have your cloak as well; and if any one forces you to go one mile, go with him two miles. Give to him who begs from you, and do not refuse him who would borrow from you."**
>
> **—Matthew 5:38–42**

A little knowledge of Roman law of that day helps. Jesus says, "Don't resist evil," but he doesn't say to lie down and let them walk all over you. His message: "Use the legal system." Roman law, under which they labored, dictated that a superior could slap an inferior with the back of the hand to keep him in place. But he could not hit him in the face with his fist. So interpreted for today, it means if someone slaps your face insultingly, you should turn the other cheek. Now he can't hit you again or you can take him to court. In other words, don't let your temper flare. Don't use force. Use your head.

The same principle applied under Roman law to a soldier's taking a person's coat. If he demanded the person's cloak as well, the soldier became guilty of forcing the person into what we would call indecent exposure. Now the person could take him to court!

And as for going the extra mile—regardless of how this phrase may have been used by pious people—what Jesus meant was to take advantage of the Roman law that said a soldier could force someone to carry his provisions and baggage one mile. But only one. If he made a civilian go two miles, he could be taken to court for abuse. So going the extra mile would have gotten the soldier into big trouble with his own superiors.[2]

---

2. The information on Roman Law is taken from the John Pilch's audiocassette program, *Stories Your Pastor Never Told You* (Credence Cassetes, 1991).

But Jesus is using the same kind of paradoxical advice martial artists have been using for years. Don't resist force with force. Let the force go further than it intended because you don't resist. Then evil spends itself and you don't increase the amount of evil.

Notice the psychological universe because it conflicts with an Eight's presuppositions. When you absorb evil instead of returning it, you will be saved by a benevolent legal system. Using the same logic on a higher level, if you absorb evil, you will be saved by the benevolence of the Father's universe. Absorbing evil becomes the means of dealing with it. Ultimately this leads to the cross and resurrection. Total absorption of evil (death) leads to total (eternal) joy. Eights have a real struggle to absorb evil because it is not fair in the short term. Perhaps some Eights can see resurrection as the ultimate revenge!

God now gives us a model on how to absorb evil. God does it not by returning evil for evil, but by the forgiveness of sins. Forgiveness is what distinguishes the search for justice from the search for revenge.

This leads to Jesus' presentation of the greatest paradox in his teaching: the kingdom in which justice will prevail is a kingdom in which sins are not punished, but forgiven. We've heard of forgiveness so often that it begins to seem bland. But against a background of repeated bloody sacrifice to atone for moral, ritual, or physical evils, it was revolutionary. Any experience of evil leads people to believe God is punishing them. When Jesus preaches a nonpunishing God and a worldview that makes sacrifice unnecessary, he frightens them. It would be like convincing inner city residents that police just make people more angry and increase crime, and recommending the abolition of the police force. People then would begin to wonder: "Who is going to deal with evil?"

The affront to the Eight's preoccupation is direct and total. The passion of the Eight is for justice, but the sin of the Eight is his addiction to vengeance. Vengeance feels like justice, just as all addictions feel like what they mimic. But from the sandbox to Bosnia, it is the common experience that if you repay blow for blow, you perpetuate violence.

Every mother when faced with a fight in the sandbox must never ask the question "Who started it?" If she does, she will initiate an infinite regressive analysis: "I hit you because you pushed me. Which in turn was prompted by my taking your truck because you wouldn't let me . . ." You get the picture. And the progression also can move forward infinitely: "You hit me so I'm going to break your house which in turn will prompt you to pour sand in my ice cream so I'll have to hide your baseball glove . . ." What is comic in the sandbox is tragic in Bosnia. American poet Howard Nemerov put it well: "The murders become memories and the memories become the sacred obligations."

Like so many forms of disordered thinking, the desire for vengeance is logical. It seems utterly sensible to punish people when they do something wrong. America believes fervently in vengeance: with the feverish building of prisons and the popularity of capital punishment, the United States makes an Eight feel right at home. And Jesus' environment was no different. "An eye for an eye and a tooth for a tooth" was meant as a type of curb on vengeance so that the reality would not become two eyes and an arm for a tooth, or a life for an insult. The real meaning was "*Only* an eye for an eye."

The only way out of the hunger for vengeance is by an act of faith. The act of faith is that ultimately the one offended will be made recompense by God. The language of the Our Father is instructive here. If you look at the Our Father carefully, all of the petitions are in the passive voice.

> Our Father, who art in heaven,
> **hallowed be thy name.**
> **Thy kingdom come,**
> **Thy will be done, on earth as it is in heaven.**
> *Give us this day our daily bread.*
> **Forgive us our trespasses,** as we forgive those who trespass against us.
> *Lead us not into temptation,*
> *but deliver us from evil.*

Everything in boldface type is in the passive voice, an Aramaic form that was called the divine passive because God was supposed to take the action. Everything in italics is what we ask of God.

Eights might notice in the most beloved prayer in the Christian world, the only thing we say we will do (in Roman type) is forgive. The rest is up to God. It is important to realize that in Jesus' vision, forgiveness is only possible because God will bring justice about. Even a powerful Eight can't bring about justice by himself.

Forgiveness can be hard for the Eight because it is passive, involving *not* doing. Everyone who has tried nonviolence knows how incredibly difficult it is emotionally, even though it may look wimpish. Eights are temperamentally and even physically oriented toward action.

But their passion for justice saves them. If they can see the futility of vengeance—it really doesn't bring justice— they can find another way to pursue justice.

When Eights (or anyone caught up in the warrior's trance) argue for the necessity of war, their first premise is that we are always going to have war. "We always have and always will. So don't even talk about nonviolence or forgiveness." On the larger screen of history, the United States and all the world powers are wondering how much vengeance to take in Bosnia. And on whom. Eights would do well to ponder the public helplessness of the military. Larger bombs don't work. More soldiers don't work. If the Eight can admit the helplessness of the warrior's solution, then other options move out of the shadows of the rocket's red glare.

The move from the search for vengeance to the search for justice is usually not possible without some appeal to a transcendent power. Prayer is essential. Forgiveness is an act of faith that vengeance will be done in such a context and in such a way that that (1) Eight doesn't have to do it, but gets satisfaction in some oblique way, and (2) the rigid trance of infinite repetition will be broken. If there is little or no confidence that the Lord will avenge the Eight, the hunger for justice will usually degenerate into the need for vengeance.

WHAT SHOULD AN EIGHT DO?

Forgiveness is central to all the Gospels. Luke concludes his Gospel with :

> Thus it is written, that the Christ should suffer and on the third day rise from the dead, and that repentance and forgiveness should be preached in his name to all nations, beginning from Jerusalem.

> —Luke 24:46–47

1. Repentance for one's own sins and forgiveness of others' sins is a summary of the whole gospel message. A good practice for an Eight would be to read this Gospel in its entirety, noting how often forgiveness is mentioned.

2. Vengeance assumes a heavy responsibility. Sometimes it may seem like an emotional response, but Eights embed a moral imperative that burdens them. The corresponding anger gives them the energy to carry the burden, but the place to start is with responsibility. They need to admit the fatigue of carrying the grudge. Eights profit from some kind of confession of their own faults. It eases their desire to punish others. Many Eights need to forgive God for their experience in an unjust world. Many other Eights need to forgive themselves. Eights can be very hard on themselves, holding themselves responsible for things well beyond their control.

3. Eights could profit from carefully studying nature. Nature is described as "red in tooth and claw," but that is a selective reading. Notice how many life forms depend on or take care of each other. Whom can you let take care of you? You are not alone.

Nines

SLEEPING BEAUTY

Nines can be among the sweetest of the Enneagram numbers. They are an emotional massage when you need companionship, warmth, and camaraderie. They don't have hard edges; they blend in beautifully. They don't make a lot of demands on you, and they appreciate what you do for them. They support and understand you, making wonderful companions. They can be like a soft summer afternoon when your only task is to find shade and stay marginally awake to enjoy yourself.

Nines are natural peacemakers, able to absorb and harmonize many points of view and sometimes huge amounts of information. They are, when healthy, extremely unselfish and include as many people as possible in their world. They don't push themselves or their agenda on you, but defer to your wishes whenever possible.

WHAT NINES WANT

Harmony or unity. Nines are variously called peacemakers or mediators, and in some traditions the Nine is considered to be the person who has not yet come to consciousness. What she really wants is to live in harmony with everyone. Along with Twos, Nines have a honed ability to merge with others. They can see all sides of a question and often have no other agenda than to get along with everyone. President Clinton, today's most famous

133

Nine, is accused frequently of listening to too many advisors, of having no clear agenda. People say they really don't know him. These are the hallmarks of the Nine. When Clinton asks Congress to work with him, you can hear the subtle Nine complaint that people don't work together enough. Nines want harmony. Their hunger comes from a background where they lived in a hostile or unpredictable environment and kept a low profile so they wouldn't get hit with flying debris. They didn't want to take sides, they just wanted to be safe and be friends with everyone.

WHAT THEY SETTLE FOR

They settle for sleep. Sometimes they sleep physically, sometimes they slump on a couch and bathe in flickering TV, and sometimes they induce sleep chemically with too much to eat and drink. They can become passive, lost to themselves, and they put themselves to sleep on many levels. Or they can stay dormant in a relationship for twenty years and wake up one morning and realize they have wanted a divorce or a different job or different home for years. They often have interiorized an environment that overlooked them and now they overlook themselves, especially regarding what they really want in their deepest hearts.

Nines have let their true self fall asleep to avoid conflict. And they are extremely angry about it. And below their anger is grief. They want harmony but harmony has to include their own voice. But in effect, they and their agenda are often absent. They make false harmony by avoidance, merging, and passivity, which denies their deepest self. Unity in this context is merely conformity. A certain cosmetic harmony prevails in a Prozac world. It resembles a flotilla of rafts all floating in the same direction. Jesus tells this parable that illustrates the Nine's predicament:

> A man once gave a great banquet, and invited many; and at the time for the banquet he sent his servant to say to those who had been invited, "Come; for all is now ready." But they all alike began to make excuses. The first said to him, "I have bought a field, and I must go out and see it; I pray you, have me excused." And another said, "I have bought five yoke of oxen, and I go to

examine them; I pray you, have me excused." And another said, "I have married a wife, and therefore I cannot come." So the servant came and reported this to his master. Then the householder in anger said to his servant, "Go out quickly to the streets and lanes of the city, and bring in the poor and maimed and blind and lame." And the servant said, "Sir, what you commanded has been done, and still there is room." And the master said to the servant, "Go out to the highways and hedges, and compel people to come in, that my house may be filled. For I tell you, none of those men who were invited shall taste my banquet."

—Luke 14:16–24

The absent guests give weighty reasons. Recent marriage, for example, excused one from the military in New Testament times. The dynamic the Nines need to hear is that the messianic banquet—a metaphor for one's relationship to God—is more important than anything else. This gets at the heart of the Nine's slothfulness. They have a certain amount of difficulty in prioritizing among social or financial choices, but waking up to their spiritual self and making the choices that support that awareness is their task of a lifetime.

The last line of the parable is a sleeper. The New Testament pattern of selection favors those who do not consider themselves invited by God. Sinners, tax collectors, Samaritans, and women are among those Jesus singles out for access to the messianic banquet. Jewish male priests and leaders were among those he challenged, annoyed, and disobeyed. He didn't do that because he had an "attitude," or because he rejected the tradition on theological grounds. He rejected the Jewish hierarchy because they were distorting the universal call to communion with his Father. Nines love a call to communion.

At the heart of the Nine's pain and grief is an absence of hope, a conviction that no such call has been issued to her. She can read this parable and legitimately identify with those who consider themselves on the outside, along the highways and hedges of life. They are called but were asleep. If they wake (and this is the term Nines use to describe breaking out of their trance), they will realize the call to communion. They have been longing for communion all their life.

The sin of the Nine is *acedia,* or sloth. The more modern word is *indolence.* He is spiritually lazy, which differs from what we generally call lazy. Nines can often be hard workers, so they don't look lazy. They are lazy about what is most important in their lives. If he really must get a report written, that may feel for the Nine like the perfect time to clean his desk, return four phone calls, write a thank-you note, shop for shoestrings, and tune his guitar.

The Nine's slothfulness is the result of an inner hopelessness. A young Nine in the third grade was told he would be put in the faster class if he got his homework done. He did the homework, was not rewarded with the faster class, and gave up—permanently. He never did well in school again. Years later, that was his explanation—he gave up because it was no use.

Nines believe their efforts are useless. Seen in this light, their attitude makes good sense. Why labor mightily in a losing cause? Einstein said the most important information to have when attempting a task is that it is possible. Nines are not at all sure it is possible.

Nines have difficulty prioritizing. When nothing substantial is possible, nothing is important. When nothing is important, neither is anything more important.

They are often late, almost as a protest against someone's saying something is important. They cling to their worldview. So when someone asks them to hurry up and do something important, they sabotage that agenda.

Many people are passive–aggressive because out-and-out aggression is dangerous and the penalties are often severe. But Nines raise passive–aggresive behavior to an artform. They have denied their own aggression so long that they are fooling themselves and others with their aggression.

Misunderstanding and confusion are often used by the Nine to frustrate people whom she wants to offend openly but with whom she is in conflict. She just doesn't understand what you mean, or she gets it perversely wrong. Pleasantly, of course.

Trying to talk a Nine into action can be like trying to pile water. Nines can smile and agree and you find out later that they couldn't do it. Why not? Oh, any reason will do, because all obstacles become insurmountable. "I couldn't fix the car because it is Tuesday and Tuesday is my day to go to the library," and so the planned trip of two months is abandoned. On the other hand, Nines may not show much remorse about staying home.

Nines can go deep into denial over where their important choices lie. In spite of their narcotic inner core, they can appear bright and happy. Ronald Reagan (a Nine) was always cheerful and happy in the public eye and appears to have been that way in private as well. (When Nines are energetic and minimizing problems, they often look like Sevens. What distinguishes the two is the deep inner lack of hope in the Nine, as opposed to the superficial optimism of the Seven. Both are in denial.)

PRIORITIES

Nines have difficulty prioritizing because of their dislike of conflict. Jesus insisted that priorities were crucial, would cost dearly, but were worth it. Nines have difficulty realizing what an act of hope it is to say that something is worth effort, that the effort will be rewarded. They might consider Peter's similar concern after Jesus told the parable of the rich ruler who was reluctant to sell his possessions and follow Jesus:

> **Lo, we have left our homes and followed you. And he said to them, "Truly, I say to you, there is no man who has left house or wife or brothers or parents or children, for the sake of the kingdom of God, who will not receive manifold more in this time, and in the age to come eternal life."**
> **—Luke 18:28–30**

Here Jesus combines the demand for commitment with the paradoxical promise that if we leave everything, we gain more—plus infinity. If this is understood literally, that is temporally, it sets one up for keen disappointment. The disciple may not get rich, famous, or whatever he wanted more than family life. Besides, if he leaves wife and family, what kind of a reward will compensate? The reward is embedded in the action of commitment. The commitment releases the energy that makes his life vital and meaningful. Wife and family are synonymous with the old way of life without Christ, so of course family and friends, in a context now made meaningless, pale alongside of Jesus' summons to life with God. On a purely psychological level, commitment furnishes the energy to leave old patterns and trances behind. This is especially important to Nines, who have a strong ability to feel one with their community. If this merging energy can be accessed, they can overcome some of their spiritual inertia.

PEACE THROUGH CONFLICT

The Nine can profit from a deep understanding of the following parable:

> **Do not think that I have come to bring peace on earth; I have not come to bring peace, but a sword. For I have come to set a man against his father, and a daughter against her mother, and a daughter-in-law against her mother-in-law; and a man's foes will be those of his own household. He who loves father or mother more than me isn't worthy of me; and he who loves son or daughter more than me is not worthy of me; and he who does not take up his cross and follow me is not worthy of me. He who finds his life will lose it, and he who loses his life for my sake will find it.**
>
> **—Matthew 10:34–39**

Jesus, whose message of peace runs throughout his gospel of healing, mercy, and forgiveness, insists that his disciples focus on him to the exclusion of other allegiances.

The context here is the identification of religion and ethnicity. The Jews were the saved people and others were unclean, offensive to God, and had a special name: Gentiles. The Gentiles were to be avoided; so were their foods, clothing, customs, language, and religious practices. They were sinners. *Sinner* today is an archaic word in a secular culture. But in a religious culture to be a sinner is the ultimate evil—sort of like being called a communist in the Fifties. We have a vivid example today in Bosnia with "ethnic cleansing," where Christian Serbs are culturally conditioned to think it is perfectly all right to rape, pillage, and destroy all Muslim Croats. The reverse is also true. This was precisely the situation in Jesus' time. In the eyes of many Orthodox Jews, to be in God's favor was only possible if you were Jewish. All others were repulsive.

Jesus talks about family relationships because Jewishness was passed on by bloodlines and Jesus crossed these. Matthew is writing to a Jewish audience who would feel this challenge deeply.

To preach peace in a context like that meant to go through conflict first. Jesus' paradox is that real peace if reached only through conflict. Nines find this terribly difficult. Entranced Nines won't face the conflict. They go to sleep, deflect attention, pay attention to everything but the conflict, talk endlessly instead of taking action, or show up at the peace talks three weeks late.

The paradox Jesus addresses to the Nines is articulated most sharply in the summarizing line:

He who finds his life will lose it and he who loses his life for my sake will find it.
—Matthew 10:39

The Nine has to experience conflict, which will feel like losing his life. Then he will find new vitality. Vitality, spiritual energy, is the promise Jesus holds out to the Nine as the reward for dying the death of conflict. The paradox goes down smoothly because we've heard it so long, but if it is taken literally, it will boggle the mind. How do you lose your life for the communion with God? Historically, this phrase has justified martyrdom, but early Christian tradition explicitly forbade deliberate choice of martyrdom. It must not be taken literally. Nor can an abstract restatement shed much light.

For the Nine it means, in a variety of concrete ways, that from a position of hopeless helplessness, one can face the pain of conflict intrinsic to the waking state. The parable says the world is not hopeless if you are a child of God, called to the fullness of life within the context of a world designed for your nurture. It is safe to come out from under the covers and walk in the sunlight. The parable insists on deepening levels that the world is a place in which trying to achieve unity with God is increasingly possible and fruitful.

Conflict is a necessary and desirable part of life. It clarifies what we want, who we are, and where we stand, and it prevents us from making wrong decisions. Conflict for healthy people is like gravity; it looks like it is preventing us from going faster, but it is really on our side. We couldn't move without it. In the process of dealing with it we become strong and vital; we develop our muscles and balance.

THE DYNAMICS OF CHANGE

When Jesus gives us parables of the kingdom of heaven, they are shot through with hope, precisely what Nines need most. The following parables have the same dynamism.

> The kingdom of heaven is like a grain of mustard seed which a man took and sowed in his field; it is the smallest of all seeds, but when it has grown it is the greatest of shrubs and becomes a tree, so that the birds of the air come and make nests in its branches.
>
> —Matthew 13:31–32

> The kingdom of heaven is like leaven which a woman took and hid in three measures of meal, till it was all leavened.
>
> —Matthew 13:33

Matthew addresses the concern that the hostile Pharisees had about the purity of the Jewish religion. The kingdom of God that Jesus is preaching will ultimately transform its context—the traditional belief that ethnicity is one's entitlement to God's favor.

The parable contains harmonics that echo in the Nine's heart. In a hopeless situation, what can you do? What did Jesus do in a situation he couldn't possibly change? He did small symbolic things and in doing these, he stirred up so much energy that billions of people have followed him.

The parables suggest a process of change for the energy-deficient Nine. If she can set modest goals and take small symbolic steps, she will release energy because her small steps are acts of hope. (The difficulty of course will be setting the goals she really wants, but if she can do that, these parables are helpful. The kind of goals that are self-defeating are the global ones like "I'm going to be myself.")

The parables also serve as a model of how personal change can be made. Regardless of how many people today may report spiritual upheavals or life-changing, ground-shaking conversions, those experiences were not the norm in the gospels. The way grace works, these parables say, is quietly. Start small with a little leaven or a seed. Then the changes have an accelerating energy that is almost self-sustaining. If a seed can become a tree, then a small change in the way we approach maintaining our car or checking account might change our lives. If a Nine asks herself to "be more focused," it's like asking the turtle to high-jump.

But if a small amount of leaven is all that is needed to transform bread, then maybe only a few actions are needed to change a workplace, family, or community. The notion of incremental change can be attractive to Nines. It will work, but only if it is symbolic—that is if the changes are on a deep enough level with clear intention and attention so that they represent the real wishes and agenda of the Nine.

Perhaps another story will illustrate the principle afresh. Once upon a time, a young man went to see a famous guru. He told the guru his plight: his life was a wreck, he didn't know what he wanted to do, and his house was especially a mess. The plaster was falling off, the floors were filthy, and the windows were cracked and dirty.

The wise guru listened and finally spoke. "No," he said, "you are not ready to study with me. I can't help you." At this the young man grew sad, but he brightened when the guru said, "But there is one thing I can do. I will give you a present. I think it will help." He then told the young man to go home, after getting his address.

The next day, the young man eagerly waited and was delighted when an exquisitely beautiful couch was delivered to his home. He had the delivery men set it up against the dirty, tattered wall. He then just sat and admired it—for a while.

He noticed the sharp contrast between the beautiful couch and the disreputable wall. So, inspired by the beauty of the couch, he cleaned up the entire wall, repaired the plaster and hung a nice picture.

Then he sat down to admire the couch with the wall. At least for a while.

Then he noticed how terrible the rest of the room looked in comparison with his fine clean wall and beautiful couch. So he got busy and scrubbed the rest of the room. It took him some time, but soon the whole room was spotless and in fine shape. He'd never lived in such elegance. He sat down to admire the room with its spotless and elegant decor. For a while.

He suddenly realized how this room made the rest of the house look. Soon, the whole house was renovated. Then the yard. Then the neighborhood, and finally the whole world!

Changes made like that are lasting and reliable. More to the point for the Nine, each symbolic act is an act of hope that confronts his distorted view of the world as hopeless. Each time a Nine confronts the distortion, armed with the knowledge that this is just a small step, she gradually wakes up to what she has missed in her sleep.

The power of symbolic change is in its ability to have consequences one doesn't expect. To live in an Enneagram compulsion is to live in a world of predictability. To the extent we are in the throes of our Enneagram type, our behavior is predictable. To the extent our behavior is predictable, our worldview has filtered out everything but what we already think we know. For example, if someone is angry, to the extent he is in the grip of his anger, all he can see, attack, or avoid is what relates to his anger. To bring up an unrelated topic will either increase his anger or simply bore him.

When we make symbolic changes, we know what the input will be. But then a transformation takes place that we hadn't counted on. In parabolic terms, we put in a seed and pulled out a tree. A seed is not a tree, it is an energy transformation system. That's what is so attractive to Nines about symbolic actions. They release energy and make changes that the Nine didn't have to program.

WHO AMONG YOU?

Jesus says :

What man of you, having a hundred sheep, if he has lost one of them, does not leave the ninety-nine?

—Luke 15:3

His introductory phrase, which we may rephrase "Who among you?" is one of the most radical phrases in religious history. It is implicitly paradoxical, because it asks you to accept the metaphorical explanation of a reality that moments before outraged you.

"Who among you?" is the difference between healthy, mature religion and cults. The phrase is practically unique among religious teachers. It has its origin in the belief system of Jesus.

The prophets prefaced their revelations with an appeal to the authority of Yahweh. They began with the formula, "Thus says the Lord." When one starts talking in the name of the Lord, one is either crazy or inspired and receives strong negative or positive attention. For the prophets, the authority of the Lord was behind them, and only to the extent that they were men of prayer and authenticity were they to be believed. Consequently, a whole set of criteria evolved over the ages about who is a true prophet and who is not.

Jesus was an authentic teacher. We believe that. His disciples believed that. He believed it. But he never used the hallowed prophetic introduction. Instead, he located authority in the hearts of his listeners. "Who among you doesn't already know what I am saying?" This simple phrase took the authority away from himself and empowered the listeners to decide for themselves.

Charismatic teachers often teach in their own name. Jesus does that once in a while. When he teaches nonviolence, for example, he says:

You have heard it said, but I say unto you . . .

—Matthew 5:21 and 5:38

But much of the time, especially when addressing the hostile Pharisees, he begins by saying, "Who among you?" and what he says is self-evident to them. But what does it mean to have something be self-evident? It means that the final authority is the listener. So Jesus either locates authority in himself or in the listener. Cults and oppressive authorities can never take the chance of saying "Who among you?" But Jesus can.

The presupposition that Jesus would have to have in order to do this, is that every listener have an inner reliable authority to make religious decisions. This inner authority, of course, is the presence of the Holy Spirit within each person. That's why if a person doesn't listen to the Holy Spirit within, there is no hope for salvation. Or as Matthew 12:31 says, the sin against the Holy Spirit can't be forgiven. The reason is that this is the source of making spiritual decisions. If that voice is silenced, there is no way to make healthy spiritual decisions.

This is helpful to the Nine who has given her inner authority away. Nines need to understand that spiritual authority resides in herself, that she has the power and the right to decide for herself what her spiritual truth is, realizing that concomitantly she has the power to carry out those decisions.

WHAT CAN A NINE DO?

1) Read the Gospel and note the passages in which Jesus places responsibility on the listeners. Also notice miracles that enable people to stand on their own two feet (healing of the lame) or see for themselves (healing the blind). Reflect on how much power Jesus gave to people to take care of themselves.

2) Notice also how much conflict Jesus gets into with his gospel of peace. Read the whole Gospel looking for conflict.

3) Make a list of things you would fight for. With whom?

4) For a month, every morning make a "to do" list for the day and prioritize everything on the list as an "a," "b," or "c." At the end of the day look at your list and see what you did. Who's in charge here?

Select Bibliography

Condon, Thomas. *The Enneagram Movie and Video Guide*. Bend, Ore.: Changeworks, 1994.

————. *Easy in Your Harness*. Kansas City, Mo.: Credence Cassettes, 1992.

————. *Waking from Trances*. Kansas City, Mo.: Credence Cassettes, 1994.

Enneagram Educator. Newsletter quarterly. Kansas City, Mo.: Credence Cassettes.

Hurley, Kathleen V. and Theodore E. Dobson. *What's My Type?* San Francisco: HarperSanFrancisco, 1992.

McKenna, Megan. *Not Counting Women and Children*. Kansas City, Mo.: Credence Cassettes, 1995.

O'Leary, Patrick. *The Art of Discernment*. Kansas City, Mo.: Credence Cassettes, 1992.

————. *Enneagram: Basics*. Kansas City, Mo.: Credence Cassettes, 1993.

Palmer, Helen. *The Enneagram*. San Francisco: HarperSanFrancisco, 1991.

Pilch, John. *Stories Your Pastor Never Told You*. Kansas City, Mo.: Credence Cassettes, 1991.

Riso, Don. *Personality Types: Using the Enneagram for Self-Discovery*. Boston: Houghton Mifflin,1987.

Rohr, Richard. *The Enneagram: Naming Our Illusions*. Kansas City, Mo.: Credence Cassettes, 1990.

Wolinsky, Stephen. *Trances People Live*. Falls Village, Conn.: Bramble Company, 1991.

PRESS

Metamorphous Press publishes books and other media for personal growth and positive change. We publish leading-edge ideas that help people strengthen their unique talents and discover how they create their own reality.

Many of our titles focus on the Enneagram and Neurolinguistic Programming (NLP). The subject of several best-selling books, the Enneagram is a fascinating powerful psychological system that describes nine personality styles that human beings favor. NLP is an exciting, practical model of communication and therapeutic change. It offers a popular set of transformational tools that enable users to change and grow in often rapid ways.

Metamorphous Press also offers selections from other useful subject areas: health and fitness, therapy, communication, self-help, education, business and sales, selections for young persons, and more. Our products are available in fine bookstores around the world and through the distributors below.

North American distributors: Bookpeople, Ingram, New Leaf, M.A.P.S. (Metamorphous Advanced Product Services)

International distributors: Airlift (UK, Western Europe), Specialist Publications (Australia), Quanta Developments (Canada)

New selections are added regularly and availability and prices change, so call for a current catalog or to be put on our mailing list. If you can't find one of our titles at your favorite bookstore, or you prefer to order by mail, we will be happy to make our books and other products available to you directly.

Please call or write us at:

Metamorphous Press
PO Box 10616 Portland, OR 97296-0616
TEL (503) 228-4972   FAX (503) 223-9117
email: metabooks@metamodels.com
http://www.metamodels.com/meta/meta.html

TOLL FREE ORDERING:
1-800-937-7771
OR CALL 1-503-228-4972

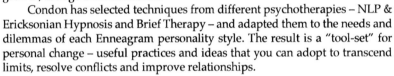

Enneagram Applications
Personality Styles in Business, Therapy, Medicine, Spirituality and Daily Life

**Edited by Clarence Thomson
and Thomas Condon**   ISBN 1-55552-103-7

Features articles by medical doctors, CEOs, pharmacists, therapists, executive coaches, corporate heads, psychotherapists, Buddhist monks, nuns, school teachers and graphologists. All have applied the Enneagram to their area of expertise and show how you can apply it to yours. Subject areas are as diverse as business, psychotherapy and self-help, medicine, literature, film, spiritual counseling and handwriting analysis. *"The delightful variety of subjects covered in* Enneagram Applications *will surprise you. I recommend this informative, practical, and enjoyable collection by highly respected Enneagram teachers and writers, including editors Thomson and Condon."* – Elizabeth Wagele, co-author of *The Enneagram Made Easy* and author of *The Enneagram of Parenting*

Enneagram Movie & Video Guide
How To See Personality Styles In The Movies

By Thomas Condon   ISBN: 1-55552-100-2

Whether you are a movie lover, aspiring actor, storyteller, student of psychology or Enneagram enthusiast, this spirited and original book will alter the way you see movies forever. From classics to independent films to mega-hits like *Titanic*, personality types are everywhere in the movies – if you know how to see them.

    The Enneagram Movie & Video Guide is a must for any reader interested in the Enneagram – or the movies. It features dozens of in-depth movie reviews plus over 1000 listings of movie characters grouped according to personality style. *"Bookstores: Get this book and display it in your store. It will be a steady seller for a long, long time."* – New Age Retailer

Parables and the Enneagram
By Clarence Thomson   ISBN: 1-55552-106-1

In this work, nationally known Enneagram teacher Clarence Thomson briefly describes the nine Enneagram styles and then offers parables designed to awaken us up from our Enneagram trance. The books unravels the teachings of Jesus in ways that will appeal to Christians and non-Christians alike. It also broadens the Enneagram by deftly and intelligently applying the system. Thomson presents parables not only for their spiritual power but also as a literary and therapeutic form. *"A masterly exploration of how the Scriptures and the Enneagram enrich each other."* — Richard Rohr, author of *Experiencing the Enneagram*

The Enneagram Spectrum of Personality Styles

By Jerome Wagner   ISBN: 1-55552-070-7

An excellent accessible introduction to the Enneagram. Offers charts, written exercises, and thorough descriptions. Includes the defense mechanisms, cognitive schemes, virtues, passions, shifts, plus the healthy and maladaptive instincts of each of the nine Enneagram personality types. A great introduction to the field, this book is both an invaluable guide for individual self-analysis and also an effective teaching aid for workshop presenters, therapists and consultants.

"It's a really good manual and I'm delighted to recommend it to both new and long term students who will benefit from [Wagner's] way of bringing the types to life." – Helen Palmer, author of *The Enneagram, The Enneagram in Love & Work.*

The Enneagram and NLP
By Anne Linden and Murray Spalding

ISBN: 1-55552-042-1

Here for the first time the Enneagram personality typing system is presented with the powerful transformational techniques of NLP. Step-by-step guidelines for an array of therapeutic interventions are given. Includes: changing limiting beliefs, transforming phobic responses, reframing, goal setting, and creating a safe environment. Enneagram therapists and NLP practitioners alike will discover valuable strategies for changework with clients. *"Necessary for all therapists, desirable for everyone else."* – Enneagram Educator

Audiotapes and CDs:
Easy in Your Harness
The Enneagram and NLP
Audio/CD Series by Thomas Condon
11 Audiotapes- $79.95 / 11 CD Set - $99.95

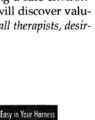

This tape series, edited from a Lifethemes workshop, is an excellent introduction to the Enneagram and offers powerful tools for therapeutic change. The presentation is a rich mixture of lecture, case histories, interviews and discussion. There are many ideas for making changes, improving relationships, and enhancing the gifts of your Enneagram style. For anyone seeking new horizons in their personal or professional growth.

To Order Call 1-503-228-4972

Enneagram Subtypes
Audio/CD Series by Thomas Condon
11 Audiotapes - $79.95 / 11 CD Set - $99.95

This new CD series, edited from an Enneagram subtypes workshop, is an entertaining, informal mixture of lecture, interviews and discussion. It is suitable for beginners as well as advanced Enneagram students.

Each Enneagram style has three further subtypes that influence people's experience of their dominant personality style. Learning about subtypes is especially useful for discovering what further motivates people within their core Enneagram style, the subtle but powerful drivers of unconscious behavior. Understanding subtypes will also help you clarify the confusing variety of expressions that can occur among people with the same Enneagram style.

The Dynamic Enneagram Workshop
Audio/CD Series by Thomas Condon
11 Audiotapes - $79.95 / 11 CD Set - $99.95

This new CD series, edited from an Enneagram Personal Change Weekend uses the Enneagram as a springboard to personal change. Featuring experiential exercises and techniques to alter negative self-images and limiting beliefs as well as change Enneagram related problems. It will help you use the Enneagram to maximize your strengths, temper your weaknesses and fulfill your true potential. To Order Call 1-503-228-4972

Dynamic Enneagram Videotapes by Thomas Condon

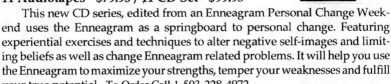

Videotapes for students of the Enneagram or those who want to learn how to apply the system's insights and diagnostic power. See the Enneagram in action as Tom demonstrates effective changework with each Enneagram style. Choose from 19 videotapes on a variety of topics. Edited from Thomas Condon's Lifethemes workshops, the tapes offer a powerful new vision of the Enneagram plus clear demonstrations of its potential as a tool for personal growth. **To Order Call 1-503-228-4972**

The Enneagram Monthly

The Enneagram Monthly, the only independent Enneagram journal and the largest publication in the field. Includes articles, interviews with well-known Enneagram teachers, news, book/movie/workshop reviews, teaching schedules. $40 a year. Call Toll Free: 1-877-428-9639 or 518-279-4444.

Printed in the United States
134487LV00002B/105/A